LIVING IN PERSPECTIVE

LIVING IN PERSPECTIVE

Facing the Enigmas of Life

Joan Gibson

Gateway Books, Bath

First published in 1989
by GATEWAY BOOKS
The Hollies, Wellow,
Bath, BA2 8QJ

Set in 11 on 12½ Andover by
Photosetting & Secretarial Services of Yeovil
Printed and bound by Wheaton
of Exeter

British Library Cataloguing in Publication Data:

Gibson, Joan, 1922–
   Living in perspective: facing the enigmas of life
   1. Life. Philosophical perspectives
   I. Title
   128'5

ISBN 0-046551-50-2

Contents

I give you the end of a golden string;
Only wind it into a ball –
It will lead you in at Heaven's gate,
Built in Jerusalem's wall.

William Blake

Introduction

Throughout the ages man has sought diligently for the precious gem stones lying deeply hidden below the surface of the earth. They can only be retrieved with difficulty and laborious effort, their rarity necessitating long and painstaking search; yet when they are brought to light, their value, their beauty and their perfection are more than sufficient reward for all the toil expended. We may notice two interesting facts about these jewels. The first is that it has taken millions of years of tremendous pressure and intense heat to form them; the second that in their raw state they can very easily be overlooked, for much of their beauty is concealed and can only be revealed after expert cutting, refining and polishing.

When we strive to understand the truth about life we find ourselves toiling in the dark, digging deeply to search for the jewels we know to be there and yet which evade our sight. Within ourselves we feel a burning desire to understand what we are and what is our destiny. We grope painfully towards a clearer knowledge of this ultimate reality, so dimly perceived, and which humanity from earliest times has found convenient to term 'God', the embodiment of absolute truth.

Life is an enigma, a mysterious state of being into which we are plunged at birth. We look about us and find no satisfactory explanation for the condition in which we find ourselves. The wisdom of the past presents us with contradicting theories, conflicting moral codes, varying religious creeds, atheism and agnosticism. Yet there can only be one absolute truth. How can we discover where it lies? The baby newly born is bewildered by all that it sees, the young child eagerly questions and wonders, seeing adults as being in possession of all knowledge, the youth is sure that he knows everything, but the old man, approaching death, can only feel how pitifully small is the sum of human understanding. We age; we crumble into death and decay. Whither do we go and whence did we come? It is as if we are opening a book in the middle and reading only one chapter. We know a very little, but so much remains a mystery.

An ancient story tells of men feasting in a king's brilliantly lit banqueting hall. A swallow flew in from the darkness outside, crossed the hall and returned into the night through a window on the opposite wall. Of such brief duration is a human life.

Yet surely we are born to discover truth; to search for it with our utmost endeavours. And, if we do so, I think we shall slowly begin to bring to light those hidden jewels which are precious beyond all price. "Seek", said Jesus, "and ye shall find." We can never discover all truth for that must lie beyond mortal ken, but it is the innate spirit of man to reach ever outward in his quest for knowledge, to understand more and more of the miraculous world he inhabits, the planets beyond it, the nature of the universe itself and of its

Creator.

To me it seems that whatever aspects of life we consider we can discern a paradox; life and death, time and eternity, light and darkness, good and evil, and so on; one contradicting and yet curiously counterbalancing the other. Perhaps in distinguishing the relationships between each we can draw nearer to reaching some glimmer of understanding. This I have attempted to do in the following chapters, trying to dig as deeply as possible into the darkness of my own dim perception in the hope that it may be of value in uncovering hidden truths. On close examination some gems may, indeed, prove to be 'fool's gold', worthless stones that merely resemble the real thing, but at least the attempt will have been made.

The treasures of truth exceed by far the value of diamonds and rubies, and we are reminded in the Bible that they are our heritage, for Isaiah wrote... "and I will give thee the treasures of darkness and hidden riches of secret places." They will not be easy to unearth, but will be well worth the seeking, for to possess these things will bring inestimable peace and joy.

1. Life and Death

Foremost of all the mysteries which surround us is that of life as opposed to death. We struggle to protect life, to preserve it at all costs, and yet without death life would be impossible. One is an intrinsic part of the other; death the price which must be paid for life. Life by dying generates life, plants supplying the necessary food to sustain the existence of animals, large animals preying upon smaller; all are interdependent. The chemical components of living creatures, whether plant or animal, are not lost by death, but recycled in an endless chain of continuing life, so that, in one respect, we may say that there is no such thing as death, if by death we mean a dissolution into nothingness.

Human life is certainly a part of this evolutionary process, but if it were only this our existence would be blank and meaningless, a bleak prospect, if we are no more than a wave in a vast sea, surging with life and individuality for a brief moment, then sinking to merge for ever into the boundless grey depths of ocean. We experience much during a lifespan which reveals something more, a different dimension through which we may travel, catching brief glimpses of something that is beyond us and yet draws us on as naturally and inexorably as a plant is drawn to sunlight.

This awareness of our true nature will only grow gradually. "What lies behind us and what lies before us are tiny matters compared to what lies within us", wrote Emerson. We begin to realise that although our bodies age, the vital self within us does not. Our emotions, loves, aspirations and longings are much the same at the age of sixty as they were at sixteen, though our bodies may by then fail us and limit our activities. To the young, the body is all-important; we exult in our vitality, strength and beauty. As we grow older we have to accept the restrictions which age imposes, but we may, if we so choose, remain young in spirit. It is futile to try to preserve the youth of the body, as some so desperately endeavour; to halt the ageing process and refuse to accept maturity. We need to consider whether we are not setting too much store on the body and overestimating its worth.

We must, of course, do all we can to keep our bodies in good health. After all, they are essential to us, as they alone enable us to live within the confines of earth. They can best be regarded, I suppose, as very complicated machines, which need to be meticulously serviced, as vital to our survival as is the diver's aqualung, or the astronaut's space suit. Yet we are as separate from them as are the diver and the astronaut, and the time will come when we may discard them as an encumbrance which we are thankful to lay aside.

We acquire our bodies at birth and so enter upon an earthly existence. To what purpose? Life is a process of learning, a progression in knowledge and understanding. Only by actually living can we experience and comprehend truths which will gradually reveal themselves to us. We know that children learn by doing; we cannot expect a baby to walk by telling him how to move his legs, or an older child to swim by giving him an instruction book; such skills are learnt by personal trial and error. We cannot prevent our young people from experiencing broken marriages or forming undesirable relationships. We must all learn wisdom from the mistakes we make along the way. And so, as we live, we learn that life can offer so much more than just eating, sleeping and gratifying our animal instincts. We discover how to love, putting the well-being of others before our own. Indeed, Robert Browning wrote that understanding the nature of love was the sole purpose of human existence. We begin to appreciate beauty, joy, peace, contentment, and to feel awe and wonder at the magnitude of creation. We are hungry for more and more knowledge and we yearn to explore the depths of the sea, the undiscovered territories of earth and the mysteries of outer space beyond our planet. We search into the history of the past to find the origins of life and we turn to religion to seek understanding of God.

We cannot achieve all this in the brief span of years which life offers us, but, however short our time and however limited our understanding, we are infinitely richer in knowledge when our journey through life on earth is over. Is this accumulation of wisdom to be lost, then, when we die and merely passed on in the genes to our descendants as a race memory? Some believe this, but to do so is to deny that there is more to life than a bodily existence, and it seems to me that so much that we experience tells us otherwise.

If we feel that life is a progression, that at its end we have built up understanding and wisdom, death, instead of being a blank wall, seems merely a door through which we pass in order to reach the next level of being. An air lock would possibly be a better description than a door. Through this an astronaut may safely pass from one atmosphere to another, shutting the first door firmly behind him before opening the next which will lead him into the place where he may shed his protective clothing, because he has now entered the air which it is natural for him to breathe. Assuredly death means a dramatic change and the closing of a door; the human body is superfluous once earthly life is over. But I think our bodies have been, at best, merely a temporary appendage, designed only to last for the short duration of our years here. If life is a continuing journey, the body may be discarded, as is a booster rocket when the space craft has escaped from the gravitational pull of earth.

If, then, our essential being, the unique oneness of personality which we all possess, survives death and continues beyond it, we may assume that life itself does not ever die, but continues in each of us. All the major religions teach that God is life itself and immortal, and it is, I believe, reasonable to think that within ourselves we all carry a spark of that divine life and, therefore, immortality. Does this, then, mean that on death we merge and are absorbed into the being of God, so losing all individuality? Again, some faiths would claim this. Christianity, however, stresses the value of the individual and the survival of the soul after death as a single entity. The appearances of Christ Himself, following the resurrection, plainly indicate, as did His teaching, that conscious life after death, while on a different plane, continues for each of us and, since we will all have acquired varying levels of attainment, it seems likely that we shall go on progressing towards a complete and perfect state of being.

Death, then, can be seen as a necessary step in our development; without it and confined to the limits of earthly knowledge we should stagnate. It is a means, rather than an end of life; a birth, just as birth itself is

an ending to whatever state we held before we entered
upon it. Birth and death are interchangeable; two
sides of the same coin. We need not fear death since we
do not have to concern ourselves with how it is to be
managed. As in birth, we can surely expect to be carried
through it by forces outside ourselves and, as in birth,
to be received into the new life with love, care and
provision for our needs. It is as natural a process as
sleep into which we enter without any qualms or
apprehension. Though we lose consciousness of the
world about us, we know that we will return to it, just
as in nature sunrise follows sunset and spring winter. It
is the normal, continuing pattern of being.

Why should we rebel against death any more than
against sleep? Both are necessary but temporary
phases. One thing we may notice, however. Day
follows day, yet each is different. Every morning holds
its own surprises, every spring its changes; the rhythm
of nature is not a monotonous, repeating cycle; it is a
spiral rather than a circle, ever advancing and developing. So death will lead us on to the metamorphosis
which would not be possible within the confines of our
mortal bodies.

I read once of a South American minnow-like fish
which is known as 'four-eyes'. This is because its large
bulging eyes allow it to see both above and below the
water. It swims just below the surface, the upper part
of its eyes being developed so as to scan the air above,
while the lower part can observe the water beneath. It
is, in effect, living in two worlds and has knowledge of
each, though it can only exist in its watery environment. If we were able similarly to develop our
awareness of a world which exists beyond our own,
death would no longer seem to thrust us into a blank
void, where all our longings, strivings and hopes would
be extinguished as casually as the snuffing out of a

candle flame.

Can the real self ever die? I think probably not, though we can certainly stunt its growth by living only for the temporal pleasures of earth and giving no thought to anything beyond it. If we each possess an immortal soul, then the body is relatively unimportant and, tragic though the death of a young person or a baby will obviously be, if we believe that life itself has continued and that we will one day be re-united, the pain of such a loss can be lessened. Such untimely deaths would be inexplicable and life meaningless, if death, at whatever age, was the final ending.

The death of someone we love seems to tear us apart with grief. Even if we believe in immortality, the loneliness can be unbearable. We feel so far from them, without any means of communication or assurance of their well-being. The faith that God is both life and love does, I think, help us to know that separation is only temporary. God is immortal, and therefore love is immortal. We can go on loving in the assurance that love is not lost by death; the love we have for them and they for us leaps over the boundary of death as if it did not exist. We may sometimes even feel the presence of those who have died, as a further assurance that death is only a curtain which hides them from our sight. If we have to go on alone for a while, we can still have their love to support us and we can extend ours to them.

We cannot hope fully to comprehend or even grasp more than a faint glimmer of the purpose of life with our limited human intelligence and experience. Certainly the accumulation of knowledge is a part of it. However, I believe that if we have a religious faith, we can begin to see the possibility of another tremendous and awe-inspiring concept. God, we affirm, is the creator of the universe, of all that we see, feel and understand. But it is a continuous creation, with all things working together to change, evolve, grow and develop. Within each created object or being, and within ourselves, we hold a fragment of God's being and His eternity. As the power of the sun begets life in plants, and plants give life to animals in an ever widening circle like ripples spreading across a pond, so we in our lives are affecting the lives of others for good or for ill. We are each a part of creation, whether we bring up children, till and make a beautiful garden, discover new ideas, work with our hands to improve our environment, or with our brains to serve our fellows. These are all small works of creation, and we are co-labourers with God. Thus our lives, insignificant though they may seem in comparison with the eons of time before our birth and the limitless distances of space, are yet of vital importance and inestimable value. In the perfection of creation every atom has its place; every life its unique and rightful function and reason for being.

Life, then, is given to us in order that we may both learn and play our part in creation; not just the creation of further life, though of course this is necessary, but also that we can put into the world something that is worthwhile, good and positive. If we can do this we are, indeed, co-operating with God, our creator, because He has extended His power into us and is working through us. We are quite free to choose whether or not our living will be positive. We can spend a lifetime taking rather than giving, but I think that if we do this we will lose the real joy of living. And living is meant to be joyful. The beauty of the earth, love, laughter, music, and the pleasures of the body are all ours and are part of the experience of life. Yet they are not the whole of it, and we are the poorer if we do not seek more of life. To hope, to search for the truth, to live creatively and to look beyond life, this will bring us treasures beside which the pleasures of earthly life will seem merely as paste jewellery. For death should be seen not as an end, but as a beginning; the next chapter to be enjoyed when we have reached the last page of the one we have written here.

I am growing ever more convinced that life and death, far from being opposites, are one and the same, but we see each from a different angle. Life is emphasised and given meaning by death: death is a transformation into a more perfect form of life. Both are our heritage; let us accept them with gratitude.

2. Good and Evil

It is very easy for us to conjecture that a perfect world would be one from which all evil was eliminated. However, if we give the matter more careful thought, we can see that human life would not be possible without some degree of pain and suffering. If we are to enjoy loving relationships, we cannot escape from grief and loneliness when they are severed by death, and were we never to experience pain or fear, we would be exposed to continual perils. Pain warns us when we are misusing our bodies; without it we would not snatch our hands away from scalding water, or exercise care when pushing through a thorn hedge. We shrink from suffering, but suffering in itself is not necessarily evil. We have to accept a measure of pain as necessary for survival. It is often a matter of proportion; many plants and minerals which are dangerous poisons when taken in excess, can be used medicinally in small quantities to heal disease. Fire and water can both sustain life and destroy it; we learn to respect and control them.

When we are young we believe that good and evil are diametrically opposed. Children speak of 'goodies' and 'baddies' in a Western film; the good men usually being distinguishable by their white hats, their opponents wearing black. In the end, good triumphs and all evil is vanquished. As we grow older, we discover that life is seldom made up of sharply contrasting black and white, rather it is presented to us in varying shades of grey; in people as well as in events, we can discern some elements of good and some of bad.

Good comes about as a result of overcoming evil. It is an active assertion of will and not a passive trait of character; indeed, many of the virtues which compose goodness; forgiveness, compassion, courage, endurance, patience and so on, can only develop through being exposed to evil. Even good health would not be appreciated had we never known illness, nor would we have any sympathy for the pains of others. Smooth, round stones are found where the shore has been pounded by stormy seas; where the water is placid, the rocks are jagged and sharp.

We may, then, accept that it is beneficial for us in life to go through turmoil at times. We say that people need to have 'the corners rubbed off'. But what of real evil as opposed to hardship or pain? How can we justify the existence of cruelty and greed, the horror of atomic warfare, the occurrence of famines, plagues and earthquakes, or the suffering of innocent children? Some feel that an all-loving, all-powerful God could not permit these things, and that, if He does so, He must necessarily be limited in power, unmindful of human life or only existing in our imagination.

Surely this is a very naive conception of God. The alternative would be for us to assume the life of mindless puppets. How grateful we should be for our freedom of will, even though we frequently make mistakes and bring misfortune upon ourselves. I believe that God does control evil, but I also believe that

He does it through us, and we are given this tremendous responsibility to work with Him in perfecting the universe. We fail continually, of course, but God has infinite patience. It is only comparatively recently that science has revealed how the world has been evolving over millions of years to reach its present state. Slowly and imperceptibly all is changing, nothing is wasted; every tiny organism has its part to play. The whole scale of creation is so vast that we cannot attempt, with a limited human brain, to grasp more than a tiny fragment of understanding. Yet, insignificant creatures though we are, to us has been given the responsibility of controlling the force of evil at large in the world. For evil is only known to mankind. The natural world of plants and animals is exposed to pain and suffering, but not to evil. Only man understands its power; only man has been permitted to choose either to cultivate it or to oppose it.

The universe is and must be governed by laws, the laws of nature, of cause and effect and chemical reaction, which are, if we have sufficient knowledge to understand them, always predictable. These laws were brought into being by the Creator of the universe for the ultimate good of all creation. In addition to these we have moral laws, formulated by man in an attempt to reach out and know the mind of God. Moral law, therefore, though good in intention, may sometimes fall short of perfection and be in error. For instance, human and animal sacrifice and the burning of so called heretics and witches, were once thought to be right and desirable. All nations and tribes have evolved their own moral codes, reaching a high level in the Jewish Law of Moses, and the highest ever attained in the teachings of Jesus. Man has within himself an instinctive knowledge of the difference between right and wrong, but he is free to disobey the moral laws which he has been taught, though, if he does so, it is against the promptings of his conscience. We are guided by God; never compelled by Him.

This awareness of evil is something we have to learn by degrees. A very young child, for instance, may play roughly with a kitten, or ridicule deformity in another child, and be completely unaware that he is inflicting pain by doing so. Evil is only perpetrated when we embrace it knowingly. Nor is it always easy to recognise good from bad when we see them in shades of pale grey or off-white. In addition to the natural and moral codes, we have the civil law, with its restrictions and prohibitions, which are often irksome but, nevertheless, essential for well-being in a civilised society. To break a civil law out of ignorance is not morally wrong, but if it is done deliberately, and for selfish reasons, then it becomes so. Civil and moral laws usually overlap; murder and theft, for example, being covered by both. But many serious moral issues are outside civil law and incur no penalty from it. Is it right, for instance, to support war? To kill is wrong, but it is equally wrong to allow innocent people to be killed or tortured and do nothing to prevent it. The choice sometimes seems to be either to uphold violence or to condone it. Another difficult question is that of vegetarianism. Is it wrong to exploit animals in order that we may live? Natural law would allow it; moral law condemns the cruelty involved. Yet were no animals bred for food many would be denied the opportunity of life at all. There is no easy answer to these problems and this is where we have to be guided by conscience, each individual being responsible for his own decision.

God does not reverse the laws of nature for our benefit, but this is not to say that prayer is unavailing. On the contrary, it is a very powerful force. Through prayer we are guided and given strength to overcome evil. God can influence our thoughts and those of others we pray for, give us opportunities to meet those who will help us, and understanding so that we know what words to speak and what decisions to make. By deepening our understanding we can learn to do God's will rather than our own. Prayer is taking our problems to God and leaving the solution to Him. Often, out of ignorance, we ask for the very things which would most harm us, as a young baby will reach out for a bright, glittering knife and not understand why his mother will deny him it as a plaything. If we can learn that God is in control, and that all is indeed working together for good, we will be able to feel peace of mind and happiness, even in a world which is torn by strife and violence and where evil seems to reign.

In God's ultimate purpose evil must be turned to good, for goodness itself is created by being set against its evil counterpart. A small child, on seeing a rose growing in manure, uprooted it to take it out of such a dirty place, not realising that from such a bed the most beautiful flowers would be produced. It has to be subjugated, not eliminated. In overcoming it and setting it under our feet, like manure in the flower bed, we are actively creating goodness and so furthering the work of God.

God does not deliberately inflict illness and suffering on us, either to test us or to punish us. Natural events like droughts, famines and earthquakes cause great distress, but in all our pain God suffers beside us and helps us to endure. It is at such times that we can see most clearly how the spirit of man can either turn towards evil or towards good. Three things stand out in my memory of film reports shown of the terrible famine in Ethiopia. I was very moved by the sight of people enfeebled by months of starvation, who yet found the strength to bury their dead with reverence and dignity, reciting prayers at the graveside according to their custom. When the pitifully small supplies of relief food were brought in, there was often only sufficient for the youngest children or those whose need was absolutely desperate. They were fed inside a wired off enclosure. The remainder watched and waited outside in patient resignation. This was a triumph of the human spirit over animal instinct, which would surely have been clamouring to break down the fence and seize a share for itself.

But the most touching story of all was told by a relief worker who was unloading a supply of corn from an OXFAM lorry. When all was gone, a few people remained to scrape up the last precious spilled grains from the floor. After they had departed a small and pathetically emaciated child appeared, but every last scrap had gone. She looked at the worker with pleading eyes, but he had nothing to give her and turned out his pockets to show that there was, indeed, no more that he could do. She went away, but returned a few moments later and handed him half a biscuit. Seeing his empty pockets, she had assumed that he, too, was starving, and as she herself had one remaining biscuit, had broken it to share with him out of pity for one who had even less. Surely these actions are the transformation of evil into good.

Of course, the reverse of this is also true. Uncontrolled and deliberately cultivated evil will destroy goodness. Unleashed it is a living power as relentless as a forest fire, which will sweep all before it. It is as deadly as poison; as corrosive as rust. Man has almost limitless powers of destruction in his hands and, if he so wills, could annihilate himself and the whole earth. Excesses of cruelty, greed, selfishness and desire for power and wealth have manifested themselves to such an extent in our own times that we feel as if we are being swept up in a great tidal wave of devastation against which we are powerless. But we need not despair. The influence for good which we individually possess is far greater than we realise. It is, as the Bible tells us, like the minute pinch of yeast leavening a vast container of flour, or a tiny seed which will grow into a great tree. Our responsibility, our purpose in living, is to set this amount of good against the evil which we see. God will further its development. We should not fear the destructive power of evil: man may well poison and destroy his entire world by abusing his knowledge of atomic energy, but this, though it would delay God's purpose, could not defeat it. Mankind's existence is measured in days and years, his entire history spanning mere centuries; God operates outside time, and for Him millions of years hold no significance at all. Good will assuredly overcome evil in the ultimate scheme of things.

Evil must exist in order that good may be achieved, but it has to be subdued and set in its rightful place. So that we may reject it and turn aside from it, we must be made aware of it and each make our own individual choice in regard to it. It is a daily choice; an ongoing development.

Being human and fallible we constantly make wrong decisions, even with the highest of intentions. It is as if humanity has been entrusted with the task of weaving a great and intricate tapestry; sometimes we set the right stitches in place, but more frequently hopelessly tangle the wools or use incorrect colours. Faulty work must, and will, be done again by others if we fail, but we ourselves can only attain true happiness in life if we are able to achieve and complete the work assigned to us.

Mankind is engaged in a lifelong struggle to create virtue from evil, forcing it into its correct position as fertiliser below the growing plant, so that its power to hurt and to destroy is not only rendered harmless, but transformed into the breeding ground of goodness and perfection. It is significant that the greater the evil, the nobler is the virtue born from it. The resurrection of Christ had to be preceded by His crucifixion.

The Nazi concentration camps of the second world war were places where evil abounded. Ravensbruck, where 92,000 women and children died, was the most infamous of all. Yet it was here that a prayer was found written on a scrap of wrapping paper near the body of a dead child:

"O Lord, remember not only the men and women of goodwill, but also those of illwill. But do not remember all the suffering they have inflicted on us. Remember the fruits we bought, thanks to this suffering; our comradeship, our loyalty, our humility, the courage, the generosity, the greatness of heart which has grown out of all this; and, when they come to judgment, let all the fruits that we have borne be their forgiveness."

3. Positive and Negative

We are often urged to think positively, and, indeed, this may be excellent advice if we have become so weighed down by pain and grief that we have ceased to experience the joy and wonder of living. But negative thinking is not necessarily bad. The path to happiness is, I believe, a middle way, for life is made up of gladness and sorrow, labour and rest, striving and attaining, sickness and health. We have to accept our share of all these and be aware of them. We cannot remain for ever on the mountain peak of ecstasy; we have also to travel through plains of the drab and commonplace. In every human life there will be a mixture of pleasure and pain, though proportions will vary, and we cannot expect an equal distribution of fortune.

It is, therefore, necessary for those who have been given a greater share of life's blessing to be willing to think negatively sometimes; to turn their attention to the pains of others and seek to alleviate them. Conversely, those who have suffered can put such experience to positive use by a sympathetic and compassionate understanding of their fellows. It is interesting to reflect that the word 'comfort' means to come alongside in order to strengthen, and that an alternative title of the Holy Spirit is the Comforter. This coming together is a combination of positive and negative, the strong supporting the weak, each being drawn to the other. We need, as St. Paul said, to "rejoice with them that do rejoice, and weep with them that weep".

The forces of nature operate by a blending of negative and positive; there must be a correct balance to sustain healthy well-being. We speak of a well-balanced person; one who is able to cope sensibly with swings of fortune, and farmers know, only too well, how extremes of temperature, too much or too little rain, lack or over-abundance of chemicals in the soil, can vitally affect the growth of their crops. We see the two forces most clearly in electricity, where positive attracts negative, and the north pole of one magnet is drawn to the south pole of another. Opposites unite, and each is necessary to sustain the other. To go to either extreme in life can be bad. A society over-loaded by hampering restrictions and prohibitions is as sickly as an over-permissive one. All sun makes a desert; all rain a flood. When the correct proportions are found then a balance is achieved; half full is the same as half empty.

We need to be aware that negative does not have to be equated with bad. There are times in life when it is necessary to be serious. Strangely enough, there can be an element of happiness even in sorrow, and to endure it is an essential part of living. Without parting we should not know the joys of reunion. "Parting is such sweet sorrow", said Juliet. Variety is, indeed, the spice of life, even if it includes a sprinkling of less pleasant experiences. We quickly become bored by a constant round of pleasures. Shelley, in his "Ode to the West

Wind", spoke of it as the breath of Autumn's being, "sweet, though in sadness", and while it presaged the coming of dark, gloomy days, he was able to say, "if Winter comes, can Spring be far behind?" Milton extolled both the joyous and the serious sides of life equally in his poems "L'Allegro" and "Il Penseroso". So often it is the negative which must come first in order to produce the positive, as in the case of the development of a photograph.

Frequently, it can be shown that what has appeared to us as negative is not so at all, because it can bring about a positive reaction. I once read a tale of, I think, Jewish origin, about a king who possessed a very large and flawless diamond which was his pride and joy. It was a perfect jewel of unique value. However, by some mischance, it became deeply scratched, to such an extent that no-one was able to repair the damage to it. Then a jeweller presented himself to the king, declaring that he could not only restore the diamond, but also increase its beauty. Doubtfully the king entrusted the stone to his care and, when it was returned, he saw that the jeweller, who was a skilled craftsman, had engraved round the ugly flaw a most beautiful rosebud, the scratch being transformed into the stem of the flower. The jewel was thus fashioned into a treasure of even greater worth than before.

I have been told that the Chinese, who are great connoisseurs of beauty, will often take the opportunity, when mending clothes, of turning a plain darn or patch into a colourful design, weaving into it a dragon, perhaps, or a flower, a sun or a moon. So the repaired garment has been improved upon and given an added attraction.

It must surely be a worthwhile philosophy of life to find in negative things a challenge to create that which is good and estimable. St. Paul claimed this to be the way in which Christ's followers should live, being " . . .

unknown and yet well known, as dying and behold we live, as sorrowful, yet always rejoicing, as poor, yet making many rich, as having nothing, and yet possessing all things", and later in the same epistle he declared, " ... therefore, I take pleasure in infirmities, in reproaches, in necessities, in persecutions, in distress for Christ's sake: for when I am weak, then I am strong".

So, it is true to say, we cannot distinguish readily between positive and negative, because the one state so often produces its opposite. Both are essential qualities of life, and we have to steer our course between them.

4. Light and Darkness

In the beginning God created the heaven and the earth, and the earth was without shape and void, and darkness covered the face of the deep, and God said, "Let there be light..."

Genesis... the birth of life, when light from the sun slowly penetrated the thick mists and darkness and stirred our planet into being. We associate light with warmth, health and vitality; indeed, with life itself. It would be possible for humanity to survive for a short time in total darkness, but only briefly, for without light there could be no vegetable matter to provide food, and without heat the earth would quickly revert to a barren, frozen wilderness in which all forms of life, even the most primitive, would become extinct. It is, therefore, hardly surprising that early man worshipped the sun, the sustainer of life and well-being, bringing to him beauty and comfort, supplying him with food and warmth after the rigors of winter: sun, the source of light, awe-inspiring and too dazzling for him to gaze upon. Light became equated with good; darkness with evil. Even today, we tend to think in this way. But darkness is as much a part of God's creation as light; it has its place, its role to play in sustaining life, and both, I believe, work together for the good of mankind.

If we try to analyse what light is, we can build up knowledge of its chemical qualities, measure its velocity, observe how various substances may react to it; colours fade, plants turn towards it, cells in our bodies respond to it, and so on. Yet we can only assess it from our limited experience in terms of what we are able to observe with human sight and comprehend with a human brain. To plants the experience of light will not be identical. Even to a blind person the concept of light must be quite different from our own, but he will still have some knowledge of it. There are blind people who are aware of lightning as a sensation which their brains can record, even though they have never experienced seeing light itself. All light, as we know it, must come from fire; either from the burning gases of the sun and stars, or from the fires which we have been able to bring about by using chemical reactions on earth.

Darkness, however, must exist in order that light may develop from it. It must precede light and sustain it. The sun burns in a great black void of space; the minutest speck in comparison to the almost limitless darkness around it. Day follows night on earth, the seasons ever changing in a regular predictable sequence. Children may fear the darkness of night, but we learn to value these hours when light fades; sleep comes more easily, the heat of day is cooled, and work may be laid aside. When a new dawn awakes us, we are ready to rise refreshed, yesterday's fears and worries set behind us.

Darkness, in its rightful place, provides much that is beneficial, and how thankful we can be to seek the shade when the weather becomes oppressively hot. The Bible speaks of the relief afforded by "the shadow of a great rock in a weary land". Farmers have frequently planted an oak or beech tree in the centre of a field used for grazing. When the tree is grown sheep and cattle thankfully shelter beneath its leafy branches, which effectively screen them from the excessive glare of the sun.

Darkness has its own qualities of beauty. Over the years I have bought three paintings which continue to give me great pleasure. All three depict sunlight; the first, a ray of morning light cast over the sea, the second, a path winding through summer downland fields, and the third, a sunny scene among the Cumbrian fells with a cedar tree by a white stone cottage in the foreground. Yet it is darkness rather than light which has given each its special quality. The shadowy gloom of the troughs below the deep waves throws into contrast the translucent light which glows through the tumbling water, dappled shadows from the hedge give depth and realism to the downland path, and the cedar tree by the cottage throws a dramatic black pattern across the road, against which the cottage and the misty fells are given a far greater prominence. Without shadows each picture would be flat and uninteresting. We should be infinitely the poorer if we had no knowledge of darkness. Lacking nightfall, we would be ignorant of the beauty and wonder of the stars, and only because of the darkness of night has their light been revealed to us.

It is the ever-changing properties of light, as it mingles in varying degrees with darkness, which gives us the wonderful roseate hues of sunset or the pure radiance of dawn. Many years ago I was, for a moment, held spellbound by evening light slanting across the northern fells, giving them, it seemed, a calm and eternal splendour which I had never until then discerned. Sunlight casts reflections, creating its own darkness, and it is these and the shadows cast by the clouds which add so much beauty to our landscape. Photographers know well the value of shadow, and shafts of radiant sunlight penetrating a dark forest or a leafy glade can be breathtaking in their splendour.

Let us consider again the quality of light. Through it we are able to perceive colour, revealed to us in its full spectrum in the rainbow. But we see light and colour only through the medium of our human eyes. Just as some animals are able to pick up sounds outside our range of hearing, might it not be possible that other colours exist beyond the ultra-violet or the infra-red? And the strange thing is that a mingling of the colours can produce both black and white. A top painted in stripes of the primary colours and spun rapidly will blend into whiteness, while an indiscriminate mixture of all the colours in a paint box will produce a blackish shade.

We cannot tell whether animals and birds experience colour as we do; probably not, though they appear to be aware of and affected by it. Flowers make use of colour to lure insects to their nectar, birds display coloured feathers to attract a mate, and insects can flaunt bright colours as a warning to predators and so protect themselves. But it may be that colours do not appear to them as they do to us. Certainly, it is obvious that we ourselves do not always see them in an identical way. How often people will argue, for example, as to whether a material is blue or green.

Light affects our mood; we tend to be more cheerful in clear, sunny weather, and the varying colours also have some influence on us; concentration on blue and green shades brings tranquillity, and over-much red aggression, while for those who are weary and depressed colours appear to fade and they see their surroundings in drab browns and greys. It is noticeable that flowers show their colours more clearly in the fading evening light or in the early dawn. Were light to remain constantly bright, we should become bored and exhausted and debilitated by it. We need its modifications, just as a varied diet is essential for the maintenance of bodily health.

I am becoming increasingly convinced that much of our experience on earth is merely a foreshadow of a far greater reality; a prototype and preparation only for what is yet to come. Our understanding of human family life enables us to begin to comprehend the meaning of the fatherhood of God; sleep and re-awaking help us to come to terms with death and resurrection. We learn to love, to feel awe and wonder in contemplating the beauty of nature; we discover music, poetry, art and literature; and through all these we begin to catch reflections of the being and glory of God: reflections only, but they are of infinite significance in our struggle to understand the truth and purpose of mortal existence.

Light, the great generator of life as we know it is, I believe, overshadowed by a far greater light which human senses can only dimly perceive, but which is to sunlight as a candle flame to a room lit by electricity. It is light superimposed on light. It is noticeable that on occasions when God has approached man, he has been conscious of a vivid light, usually described in Biblical accounts as "the glory of the Lord". Moses saw it in the apparently burning bush; a pillar of fire guided the Israelites by night, the Bethlehem shepherds were overawed by it, Paul was temporarily blinded by it; a light brighter than the noonday sun. It shone from the face of Jesus after the Transfiguration, and we are told that God Himself is light: not the light of the sun, but the light of truth, love, pure goodness and ultimate reality.

This is the Light of the world; the light that guides, illuminates and strengthens us. We can experience it for ourselves: it does not merely occur in strange, supernatural incidents which we read of in the Bible. Few, of course, will feel its impact as strongly as Paul or Moses, but nonetheless, there are times when momentarily we may be aware of the presence of God.

I have, myself, a very clear recollection of a warm summer day when, sitting alone reading under a shady tree, I looked up and was suddenly conscious of being encompassed by a wave of radiance, warmth and love. The moment quickly passed, but left with me a sensation of perfect happiness and peace. At such times, I think, we are very close to God. We may experience something similar when we enter a great cathedral or an ancient church where prayers have been said through many centuries. There is an indefinable sense of peace and joy which, for an instant, lifts our spirits, so that we are in touch with, not so much light that we can see, as with lightness of being; the light of God's presence.

We often associate light with both sight and knowledge. We need light in order to see, and 'I see' frequently means 'I understand'. We see with our minds, and our minds, though guided by the observations of our eyes, do not necessarily depend on them. People born blind can still reason and comprehend. By making use of their other senses, they learn to assess the world, and though limited to some extent, they can often so develop alternative faculties, as to live as fully and advantageously as their sighted colleagues.

It is possible to appreciate a rose by touch and smell and to gain more pleasure from it than those who, seeing it, are yet unmoved by its beauty. God, as the Light of the world, can reveal to us if we are willing, things that exist but have been hidden from us by the darkness of ignorance, prejudice or superstition. It is in this sense that we speak of the Dark Ages, the dark continent, darkened minds, and so on. We have, of course, to remember that darkness itself is not destructive; the contents of a room remain the same whether we enter it at midnight or during daylight hours, but at night we may be unaware of what it contains. The fabulous treasures of Tutankhamen's tomb lay buried and forgotten for many centuries, and when it was finally discovered and the darkness of the innermost chamber broached, it was the light of a torch, infiltrating the burial place through a crack in the wall, which revealed to the wondering eyes of Howard Carter and his fellow archaeologists the glint of gold and jewels within.

It seems to me that darkness is necessary and advantageous and that we have no cause to fear it. Light and darkness are two sides of the same coin, alternating for our benefit. Light can always overcome darkness and reveal all that it conceals. Similarly, the light of knowledge is there to guide us, as surely as a powerful torch will light up the road on a moonless night.

Light and life are almost synonymous, and both alternative names for God. Similarly, we may couple darkness and death, and fear neither, for both the pairs are counterparts, the one bringing forth the other. A line of a hymn expresses this when, speaking of God it declares, "for dark and light are both alike to Thee".

Being made aware of both light and darkness, our purpose in life is to distinguish between them, to seek the light and travel towards it as a plant turns to the sun. Darkness will still be there, but if we face the light our shadow will fall behind us and we will see with a greater clarity the way ahead. This using of darkness in order to create light is shown in the prayer:

Lord, let me use disappointment as material for
patience,
success as material for thankfulness,
suspense as material for perseverance,
danger as material for courage,
reproach as material for long-suffering,
praise as material for humility,
pleasures as material for temperance,
pain as material for endurance.

5. Science and Religion

It is widely supposed that science and religion are in opposition; that the scientific mind can find an explanation for life and its origins which precludes any necessity for the existence of God, and that the religious dismiss logical thought in favour of myth and superstition. This, however, is a misconception, for science and religion have a single, common aim; both are searching for the truth.

The difference lies in their approach to that search. Science adopts the negative attitude, admitting no fact unless it has been proved correct; religion the positive stance, assuming that God exists, and from that premise looking for evidence of His existence by means of instinct and faith rather than by logical reasoning. It is as if both were travelling towards truth from opposite ends of the same line and, since the truth each seeks is the one and only truth, they will eventually meet, having reached an identical goal.

To come to a true understanding of life we need, I think, to follow each of these roads. Because we are human and fallible the paths of both religion and science have, through the ages, often taken a wrong turn. We do not now believe some of the early religious teaching, for example that God requires human sacrifice, or that heaven is a region set just above the clouds, with our earth the centre of the universe. Similarly, errors have been made in scientific thought; how long, for instance, the world has been in existence, and the belief that the atom is the smallest possible particle of matter and indivisible. Slowly we discover and build up our knowledge, discarding old and outdated theories as we learn more about ourselves and the world we inhabit. There is, and can only be, one truth and we grope towards it continually, for the enquiring mind is an essential component of man and our purpose on earth to learn and to discover.

I believe that the world is still in the process of creation. That God planned and made a perfect earth which somehow became perverted by man's sin and slipped from His control, would seem to imply that God is not all-powerful and can be overcome by evil. Evil undoubtedly exists and is a terrible and destructive force, not in the world itself, but in the heart of mankind. To control and to subdue it is our task, our paramount reason for being entrusted with life, for God is continuing His creative work through us.

We fail continually; we are misled, deceived, mistaken, indifferent, or we may even deliberately choose an evil way of life. Yet every good, positive and constructive thought, word or action in our lives is forwarding God's purpose, bringing nearer that time when, as the hymn says, "the earth shall be filled with the glory of God, as the waters cover the sea". And it is, I believe, our tremendous privilege to be God's instruments in achieving that perfection which is yet to be. We are guided by God in this, taught and shown the example of a perfect life by Jesus, strengthened by His spirit; and

He is allowing us, puny, unworthy and feeble creatures as we are, to bring about His will on earth.

It is a frightening and awe-inspiring thought. How can we influence the destiny of mankind? We feel that we are utterly powerless to prevent war, atomic disaster, the rise or fall of political regimes, the corruption of the young by drugs or crumbling moral standards, and yet this is not so. Just as single drops of water together compose the ocean, so what we do as single individuals is vitally important in the complete scheme of things. Our thoughts, our aspirations, our positive actions, will influence others for good or for ill; not one life will fade into nothingness without leaving behind some trace of its passage. We build or we destroy, the choice is ours, but we can never be neutral, and I believe that if our search after truth is carried out sincerely and conscientiously, then we can indeed bring nearer the time when all truth is known and understood.

The sum of mankind's knowledge is pitifully small. Despite the accumulated wisdom of the ages, the advance of technology and scientific thought, psychological research into the human mind and the wisdom of philosophers, we are still baffled by the enigma of life. As we contemplate the immensity of space beyond our planet, our minds are numbed by the sheer magnitude of it all. We feel of as little account as a single speck of dust. And yet religion tells us that, to God, each human life is of infinite worth; and science that it is all-important to work tirelessly to push back the frontiers of knowledge, reaching ever further into the unknown.

Knowledge is not always identical to understanding. We can know how to drive a car without understanding the complexities of the engine. We may use electrical appliances and computers, enjoy the benefits of radio and television and yet have little comprehension of the intricacies of their composition. Similarly, religion claims that we can know God, yet not understand Him. Science is more cautious and, while it does not deny God's existence, it makes no claim to acknowledge Him. Yet science and religion both venerate truth, and to the religious God is Truth.

Here we come to the conflict between faith and doubt. It is healthy, and indeed right, to doubt. Faith is not a blind acceptance of dogma laid down by our teachers, parents or the church. That kind of faith collapses at once when faced with hardship, pain or persecution. Neither is faith the belief in a God whom we have manufactured to suit our own inclinations. It is so easy to make God in OUR image, rather than the other way round; early man did just that, picturing his gods as a species of supermen, who could be angry, jealous, vengeful, greedy and capricious. We still form our own conception of the God we worship, and we must be prepared to revise that image if necessary as we learn to understand His nature more fully. We cannot worship a make-believe God. We must not be afraid of the truth; and it is here that we find the scientific approach helpful. We test, and try and reject that which we discover to be untrue. Religion teaches that we instinctively reach out for God, because this is as natural to us as migratory birds returning to their nesting places. It does involve taking a leap in the dark, certainly, but knowing as we do so that we are in His care. Science uses doubts to produce positive facts. Religion uses doubts to build up faith. Both lead us to the truth.

Science and religion are rather like the sisters Mary and Martha of Bethany. Both do work that is necessary, and both sisters held a special place in Our Lord's affection. Yet, just as Jesus said that Mary had chosen the better part, so it is religion that will bring us closest to God. For God is far greater than our understanding and we learn to know Him, not through scientific facts, but in simple intuitive feeling, turning to Him instinctively as a baby to its mother. We learn of God by our experience of living, we seek truth, love and goodness and find that God is all of these and, believing this, we are able to overcome our doubts and fears and trust Him to care for us and protect us. We are not, because of this belief, immune from sickness, pain, suffering or evil, but find that we have strength to overcome them. Religion offers us no proof, but we do not have to take our faith on trust alone. "O taste and see that the Lord is good; blessed is the man that trusteth in Him", wrote the psalmist. For many, the beauty of the earth is sufficient proof of God's existence, and Keats declared:

> Beauty is truth, truth beauty, that is all
> We know on earth, and all we need to know.

However, this cannot be seen as a conclusive argument. There are those who will deny beauty, such as the cynic who saw flowers merely as the gaudy sexual organs of vegetables, as, of course, they are, and yet how much more. We must not be afraid of our doubts. Rather we must face them honestly, use our brains, our instincts and our experience of life to build up the faith which we believe to be true, because, ultimately, truth alone is the only thing which has any significance or meaning.

6. One and Many

It seems to me that much that is perplexing in life can be better understood by a study of nature. Here, individuality and unity can often be seen as coinciding; the sea is made up of single droplets blending into one, a mantle of snow by an accumulation of snowflakes; even more clearly this is illustrated by considering a drift of bluebells under the trees, beautiful as a whole, yet each flower unique and perfect in itself. Every tree which makes up the forest has its own specific characteristics, shape and form. Throughout nature the individual is complete and distinctive in isolation, yet blends and merges to build up a different whole of which it is merely a component part.

This is seen in the behaviour of birds; each fiercely defends its own territory and, while co-operating with a chosen mate to build a nest and rear its young, is independent of the rest of the species. Yet we also observe a remarkable unity among birds. A flock in flight will rise, wheel and settle simultaneously, as if linked by telepathy between them, and in migration huge numbers will follow an identical yet featureless path over seas and deserts.

Most insect and animal life pursues a similar pattern, each living for itself, yet grouping within its own kind for protection or mutual convenience. It is interesting to note that in a few cases a collective noun may be the same as that used for an individual. Thus we say that we saw the sheep or the deer, meaning either a single animal or a group.

Individuality is something on which we all set a high value. It is an amazing fact that no two people on earth can be identical in looks or in character. The Buddhist ideal, the state of nirvana, in which separate personality merges into a cosmic whole, holds little appeal for the majority of us. Yet, despite this, it is a human characteristic to conform; to follow the customs of our peers, in clothes, manners, speech and actions. To stray too far from the norm is to be labelled an eccentric or a freak. Here, too, in nature we see the mutant shunned by the rest of its kind. It is curious that whilst young people tend to dislike wearing school uniform because they wish to be free to dress as they please, when allowed this freedom they will slavishly follow the accepted fashion trends and choose almost identical hairstyles and clothes to those of their colleagues. While we enjoy indulging our own particular idiosyncrasies and like our homes to some extent to express our own personalities, we nonetheless so often feel impelled to 'keep up with the Joneses'.

In some strange way it seems that we are drawn to one another. Although it is possible for a human being to live a solitary life, complete isolation for a long period is very hard to bear and we are happier if we can maintain contacts with each other. Most of us find our greatest satisfaction and happiness in marriage; a good marriage brings about a blending of personality, traits in one partner complementing those of the other. Yet, for a marriage to be truly happy, some individuality must also survive; areas of privacy, diversity and freedom which each will respect. The drawing together of human minds can often be seen most clearly in twins, when both may experience identical emotions, and it is certainly true that telepathy can take place between one individual and another if their personalities are, as it were, attuned. We all carry in our inherited genes race memories of the past, so that we are not wholly ourselves alone, but are influenced by our parents and our ancestors whose characteristics are part of our own make up.

We possess a single body, unique to us; yet that body is made up of millions of cells, each one of which is different, yet each constructed in the same way. Every cell, minute as it is, resembles a tiny universe with electrons being drawn round a central nucleus, as planets revolve round the sun. This strange conception of one yet many runs through the whole scale of creation.

When we consider this idea of blending and dividing, we may visualise yet another possibility. Could it be that the personality we so jealously guard as being our own and entire to ourselves has already been fragmented, and that other aspects of ourselves co-exist in the world or in alien worlds? If this were so, we should not be complete beings until all these elements of ourselves were re-united, which would perhaps occur after death. Such diversity might be beneficial, allowing us to meet with a greater variety of human experiences. I do not, myself, think that this is probable, but it is not an impossibility. We often fail to understand ourselves, and it is certainly easy to deceive ourselves. This is why we are so poorly qualified to judge others, and one lifetime seems all too short a period in which to probe the complexities of the human mind.

It seems to me that both the 'one' and the 'many' are necessary to build up the whole. There is a story told of a man playing a piccolo in a great orchestra, who felt that his part was so insignificant as to be worthless. During one rehearsal he remained silent when it was time for his few notes. At once the conductor brought the orchestra to a halt. "Something is missing", he said. "Where was the piccolo?" Many do need to blend together, but for that blending, individuality is essential. The words of the Communion Service express this thought; "though we are many, we are one body, because we all partake of the one bread".

Referring again to nature, we discover that when two substances merge it may be possible for a third to be created. Blue and yellow will combine to make green, a colour which could not exist without the two primary colours, and yet it is a colour in its own right and quite different from them. Copper and tin together will produce bronze, and, of course, male and female must unite before a child of a species can be born.

It is by first understanding these principles that we can better comprehend the nature of God, who is one and indivisible; and yet is also Father, Son and Holy Spirit; He is in us and we in Him.

7. Male and Female

All sentient life on earth, apart from the very simplest, exists in two separate forms, the male and the female. Each complements the other, and they must combine for the purpose of reproduction. These are elementary biological facts. But when we come to our own species, male and female characteristics are more complex, and both now and in the past there have been conflicting opinions as to the role to be assumed by either sex.

In animals and plants there seems to be little deviation. Male birds and animals almost always assume the dominant role, displaying brighter colours or more distinctive features to attract the female. Variations of this may sometimes be seen in the insect world, of course. The drone bee is smaller and less active than the queen, his sole purpose being to mate with her; while the neutral workers accomplish the necessary work of the hive and its protection. Occasionally the female insect will be the more aggressive, as in the case of the mantis, which is believed frequently to kill the male after mating. But these characteristics remain consistent in each species.

In man it seems that the roles played by male and female often change or merge together; what is acceptable during one period of history or in one culture being rejected in another.

In early times the fertility of woman was given great prominence. The mother figure became venerated, a mother goddess or earth mother was worshipped, and fertility rites and superstitions were prevalent, but, even so, women themselves usually had a very subservient part to play in the community. There were a few exceptions, however. A priestess in ancient cultures could command awed respect from both men and women, and it was by no means uncommon in the older civilizations, such as the Egyptian, for a woman to assume a despotic rulership.

In our own history it has only been comparatively recently that women have begun to seek to free themselves from the need to be dependent on men. For many centuries an unmarried woman would feel shame at being a burden to her family, for there were few means by which she could support herself. The two world wars were largely responsible for the opening up of many types of work for women. With most available man-power directed into the armed services, it was sheer necessity that made the country turn to women to carry on the essential work on the home front.

So, for the first time, women began to take on jobs which had formerly been the prerogative of men alone. Even earlier, women had entered the nursing profession during the Boer war. Now they became doctors, office and factory workers, farm hands and even mechanics, drivers and road sweepers. Work with children had, naturally, been acceptable for women in the past, and the wealthy had been able to employ maids and housekeepers, but the idea of women continuing work after marriage was disapproved of, except in the case of a married couple being engaged as servants. In the teaching profession, for instance, only single women took posts, whereas today they are far outnumbered by their married colleagues.

The demand for equality between the sexes began, in this country, with the passionate desire of women for universal suffrage, but has in our own times, I think, reached rather ridiculous proportions. For men and women are fundamentally different and can never reach complete parity. Life would surely be rather dull if they did. It is indisputable that most men have greater physical strength; most women an instinctive desire to mother and protect. We all possess characteristics of both genders to some extent, but women naturally have a preponderance of female attributes, and men of male. Homosexual tendencies in a man may sometimes arise when there are a higher proportion of female traits than the norm, or when the masculine is suppressed. Lesbianism in women can occur for similar reasons. Although this is no longer regarded as shameful, and rightly so, it must obviously fall short of the normal heterosexual way of life.

Of course, it may sometimes be necessary for us to take on the role of the opposite sex. A man may be left, on the death of his wife, to bring up young children and will not find the task impossible; a woman can learn the art of self-defence and successfully foil the assault of a man twice her size. However, the natural reactions of men and women are not identical. It is said that confronted by imminent danger of attack, a man will instinctively protect his head, and a woman her stomach.

The most perfect and natural state attainable is that of marriage, where both male and female unite to create a whole entity, each contributing to the other while still maintaining their individuality. This is the ideal, but we know, only too well, that not all marriages can achieve it. In contrast, though, we can also see that celibacy is by no means an inferior way of living, and for many the monastic life has proved to be an entirely fulfilling vocation. In any case marriage on earth can only be a temporary state "until death us do part".

When two young people fall in love and marry, their future happiness together is by no means automatically assured. They are taking the very first steps into a completely new phase of life where their two personalities will blend, where, as the Bible says, "they twain shall be one flesh". No longer will they live as self-seeking individuals, but if the marriage is to succeed they must learn, step by careful step, to merge their separate beings physically, mentally and spiritually. In an ideal marriage this is achieved, not by one becoming subservient to the other, but by each contributing positive qualities which will combine into a new whole. In such marriages the partners will blend their lives together so harmoniously that friends will, almost subconsciously, regard them as a pair, rather than two separate people; yet, far from being diminished, the life of each will be enriched and made complete. Few, in fact, can attain such an idealistic marriage as this, but we can come close to it, and it is the goal on which to set our sights.

It seems to me that life demonstrates to us that a balanced whole is best gained by this merging of male with female. But life on earth can never reach a state of entire perfection. Perfection, that is absolute beauty, truth and goodness, is found in God alone. We are drawn towards it, as iron filings to a magnet, throughout our earthly life. It must be our aim if we are seeking fulfilment and purpose in being, rather than aimlessly drifting through the days. "Be ye perfect", said Jesus, "even as your Father in heaven is perfect".

We are promised that perfection, but will find it beyond the confines of this life, where too much in ourselves, and in the world around us, is distorting the clear vision of that truth and beauty. We may catch brief glimpses of it, and this will encourage us on our journey. Perhaps, as small children, we have an even clearer insight when, as Wordsworth said, "trailing clouds of glory do we come, from God who is our home".

It is said that it would not be possible for there to be standards of utter perfection on earth because our own flawed natures would be unable to bear them. If, for example, musical instruments could be tuned to an absolutely true pitch, our ears would not be sensitive enough to register it as such and it would sound discordant, so even our most lovely music tends to be very slightly off key. Were God to reveal Himself to us, our mortal eyes would be blinded by His radiance.

When one partner in a marriage dies the other should not feel utterly alone and bereft, for all, I am convinced, that has been built up in their union can be continued beyond the temporary barrier of death. Naturally there will be mourning, but the loss is not irrevocable and for ever. In this world we join in physical union; in heaven that is unnecessary, for mind and spirit will there be able to blend in perfect harmony.

It is obvious enough that nature uses the combination of the sexes to produce new life, that this union is a source of pleasure and that, in caring for the young, two parents will be better able to ensure their protection. However, I think we can see a deeper reason for the differences between male and female if we look beyond the confines of this life which is but a preparation for a greater life ahead of us. All that we learn here will have significance, just as children here learn in school how to cope with adult life. By living, we discover how to love and care for others rather than only ourselves. The attraction between the sexes leads us on towards such love and has often seemed to me a learning aid, just as an abacus will help a small child to count. Once the skill is learned the aid becomes superflous. There will, I am sure, be no deprivation in finding that heaven lacks sexual intimacy, for men and women will be as one and will yet be able to give themselves to each other in perfect love.

I have never been able to understand the controversy as to whether God Himself is male or female. How can He be either? Differentiations of sex within a species exist on earth only, as does our notion of time as opposed to eternity. If we think of God in earthly terms, we are trying to form Him in the image of man, not understanding that it is we who are in His image, and so destined to grow into His perfected concept of us. When Jesus became Man He brought Himself down to our level, and so is able to meet the needs of all mankind, both male and female equally, since, as God, He makes no distinction of gender. We speak of God as 'He' in the sense that 'mankind' includes both man and woman, because our language has no other pronoun to express this state of being.

Whether or not we marry on earth is not necessarily important, since marriage in heaven will be of mind, not body. Male and female can, however, be seen as essential parts of the whole being which we will one day become. We have to experience both masculinity and femininity within ourselves, so that they will merge, as ingredients in a recipe, to form a new and more complete creation.

Thus on earth male and female are complementary factors within creation, working together to form us into the true being to which we shall eventually evolve.

8. Success and Failure

It is all too easy for us to assess the lives of others and to say that they have been successful or that they are failures. We are poor judges. So often we look at one aspect only; our standards are very different from God's.

When the prophet Samuel was seeking a future king for Israel, he considered seven of the sons of Jesse and his first instinct was to select one of them, but later he came to realise that they were unacceptable to God, "for the Lord seeth not as man seeth; for man looketh on the outward appearance, but the Lord looketh on the heart". Thus David, the youngest, who had seemed the most unlikely candidate, was anointed.

We can readily distinguish between success and failure in certain events, for example, we can either win or lose a game; but when it comes to life, or experiences in life, it is a different matter and the two can become confused. As adolescents we consider our aims in life and, if we are lucky, we are able to embark on the career of our choice. More frequently, we encounter barriers from the outset. We may have to accept long periods of unemployment, lack of promotion, or disappointment in what we are able to achieve. We enter upon marriage with high and romantic expectations, only to find areas of disillusionment and, perhaps, even boredom as the years pass. It is only as we grow older that we begin to understand how naive were our youthful dreams, that success is seldom presented to us on a plate, but can be brought to fruition only by travelling first the path of failure and loss.

We each possess within ourselves the potential to attain that for which we were created; our own personal mountain peak. Sometimes it takes a lifetime to discover what this may be and we may never reach it, but this I think, for us, is the ultimate success or failure. Fame in the eyes of the world, in the spheres of art, music, literature or learning, to be acknowledged as a leader, to amass great wealth, or to be remembered in history for acts of heroism, is the destiny of only a very few. Those who do not surmount these heights have by no means failed, for they have other roles to play. But each of us has a unique place and we are responsible for fulfilling that potential which is ours alone. We have to set our own goal in life and seek to gain it. The path which leads to it will be beset by difficulties, for life is made up of a succession of victories and defeats, both small and great. We learn this from our schooldays onwards, and we also learn that success is only won after a series of failures. We have to fall off a bicycle many times before we can ride confidently along a busy road.

It is very easy to have a false conception of success in life. If we deliberately set ourselves a low target which is far below our capabilities, we may well accomplish it, but would have little cause for self-congratulation. The man who was entrusted with one talent and buried it in the ground was able to present it intact, but had made no effort at all to increase it and earned condemnation rather than praise. Similarly, a man who aimed to climb the foothills could achieve this with very little exertion, but a dedicated climber, who struggled all his life to scale Everest but never quite attained the summit, would surely be worthy of far more credit. He, of the two, would be judged to have won a greater victory. Browning made this very point in his "Grammarian's Funeral". Apparent failure can prove to be success; a lofty aim not fully realised is preferable to a feeble one too easily perfected.

Yet we are ill-equipped to make judgements or to estimate the value of a human life. The standards we apply may be faulty in themselves. Because a young woman is selected as 'Miss World' in a beauty contest, she cannot therefore assume that her comeliness surpasses that of every other living woman, unless the entire female population of the earth had competed with her. Even then, the choice would depend on the judges' preconceived notions of beauty. That which is deemed to be noble and great may well have hidden flaws, and much that is worthy may never be recognised. As Gray pointed out in his Elegy, there are many unsung heroes and countless forgotten saints. Nor does a long life with a succession of achievements necessarily merit great praise. "A lily of a day", said Ben Jonson, has fulfilled its purpose on earth as equally as the oak which has endured for three hundred years.

In life many apparent successes prove to be quite the reverse. In one of Aesop's fables a dog carrying a large bone caught sight of his reflection in the river. Supposing this to be another dog, he opened his jaws to seize the rival's bone also and, in doing so, the one he was carrying fell into the water and was lost to him. Greed for material possessions can deceive us into thinking that by amassing riches we are living successful lives. We may, indeed, gain such wealth and in the process lose much which is of far greater value. I have been told that in North Africa, tribes wishing to catch small monkeys have found an easy method of trapping them. A gourd is hollowed out, with a hole in its side just large enough for a money to insert its paw. The gourd is then filled with nuts and left tied to a tree. A monkey will approach, smell the nuts and push in its paw to seize them. However, the hole is too small for it to withdraw its fist. Were it to relinquish the nuts, of course, it could do so, but being unwilling to leave such a valuable prize, it remains and is easily captured by the hunter.

We do need to ensure that the goals we set ourselves are really worth attaining. Napoleon and Hitler became great leaders, feared or venerated by thousands of their contemporaries. Yet both died dishonoured and embittered men.

Just as apparent success may result in failure, so the reverse can be true. Hans Andersen's ugly duckling was convinced that he was sadly deficient when he aspired to grow into a duck; naturally so, since he was destined to be a swan. Frequently our aims in life are pitched too low. We need not fear to reach to the stars. Christopher Columbus, Scott of the Antarctic and Moses all attempted gigantic ventures and all failed; yet, by their very failure achieved greatness and paved the way for others to follow in their footsteps and reach the goal they sought.

When we look back over our lives we frequently find that events which had seemed disasters at the time have turned out to be blessings in disguise. Left to ourselves, we would have made ill-advised choices, but circumstances have forced us to change direction and eventually good has come out of the very situations which we had found so irksome and hard to bear. The

Biblical concept of God as a shepherd and ourselves as sheep is so apt. Like sheep, we instinctively follow where the majority lead, and like sheep we easily panic, lose our way and wander into the very predicaments which will harm us most. Sheep in snowy weather will seek refuge from the bitter cold and often choose hollows sheltered from the wind. Here they will apparently be safe, but the shepherd knows that these are the very places where the snow will collect in great drifts and where they are most likely to perish. He goes out on the hillside to find them, driving them from such hiding places out into the open again. No doubt the sheep resent this and feel that he is being cruel and uncaring. They do not understand that he is taking them out of danger and back to the sheepfold where they will be secure. So often we are angry with God for apparently denying us the comfortable lives we would choose. We have to learn to trust Him to direct us. It is not easy to be able to say:

> For all the heartaches and the tears,
> For gloomy days and fruitless years,
> I do give thanks, for now I know
> These were the things that helped me grow.   *Anon*

But when we understand this we begin to see more clearly the true purpose of our lives.

I recently saw a television programme on the English Lake District, to my mind the most beautiful place on earth, with its majestic fells, still, tranquil lakes, tumbling becks and patchwork of green fields interlaced with dry-stone walls. The programme traced the evolution of this region through millions of years. First came the fiery volcanoes spewing out molten lava, then a great arid desert where nothing could live, followed by an age of ice and huge glaciers, which slowly and relentlessly carved out valleys through the rocks and

scattered giant boulders across wasteland as barren as a
lunar landscape. Then, slowly, plant and animal life
became possible, and the matchless beauty we see
today began to come into being, created out of what
had appeared to be the mindless chaos and confusion of
those long preceding ages.

Perhaps learning to fail is the most valuable lesson of
all. It may even be that we need to experience failure
before we can truly succeed in our life's task. We have,
after all, to teach our children how to lose in a game, to
be able to accept defeat without resentment, and to be
willing to try again with cheerfulness. So, in life, we
must expect frequent rebuffs and disappointments and
not be deterred by them. Sometimes, indeed often, we
will fail in what we have sought to achieve, but out of
that failure we can, if we will, find the seeds of success.
We need to discover what was wrong in the failed
attempt and, having learned from it, go on to try again.
Success always comes, but it may be long delayed, and it
may be in an entirely different form from our original
conception of it. It could even be that seeming failure in
life will be the greatest success of all. This we have to
leave in the hands of God.

9. Time and Eternity

What do we mean by these two words? They are by no means easy to define. Time, we may say, is a sense of history; a sequence of events which have occurred in the past or may happen in the future. We visualise it, perhaps, as a line having a definite beginning and end, intersected by events which cross it and are spaced out in exact chronological order. Eternity we see as a line also, the end of which, like the horizon, goes ahead of us and, however far we travel, can never be reached. Events, then, such as the coming into being of our planet, a definite happening which at some point took place, must likewise intersect the eternity line.

But something seems wrong with these theories; a line, however long, must start and end somewhere. The reason for the receding horizon is the circumference of the earth, and this has led some to suppose that eternity must be a circular line which would thus have no beginning or end. There was an ancient belief that eon would follow eon in a continuous, repetitive circle, with every so often an 'age of gold' or perfection arriving, after which the whole cycle would recommence. Nature does not bear this out. We do see cycles of events in the world about us; the changing seasons, and the movement of the planets round the sun. Yet, despite this, nothing is ever exactly repeated; the years have slight variations in climate, and there are slow but subtle changes throughout the solar system. The sun is gradually cooling; nothing remains constant. Quietly but persistently all is evolving and developing.

A little more credible is the notion of eternity as a spiral; circling it is true, but each circle rising slightly higher than the preceding one. Even so, a spiral is still only a coiled line and must have a beginning and eventually come to an end. It cannot be a true picture of eternity.

I have often thought that a very young child has a far clearer understanding of time and eternity, for he sees them as one and the same. He lives in the 'now'. He knows nothing of death, nor does he remember his birth. For him existence will continue unbroken as it appears to him in the present. Children are heedless of the passage of time; unlike us, their lives are not ruled by the clock. They do not try to re-live the past or worry about the future.

We are apt to over-simplify our idea of time, I think, for we assume that it stretches far ahead of us. Yet life is unpredictable and can come to an end suddenly and unexpectedly. We cannot count on the future, for all our elaborate forward planning. Just as we are unable to take in food or air in large quantities to stock up for a week ahead, so we cannot take for granted that our own lives, and therefore our own allocation of time, will continue indefinitely. We sometimes speak of people living on borrowed time, but, to an extent, we all do, for we do not possess time; it is ours only for the length of our existence on earth. Each moment is a gift, not a right.

Let us, therefore, consider time and its relationship to us. We measure it both by the ageing process of our bodies and by the movement of the earth in association with the sun and the moon within our solar system. Time is thus very much dependent on a particular planet and the conditions of life upon it. It would seem completely different in galaxies other than our own. If it were possible to be both outside our bodies and any planetary system, time would be meaningless. This then would be eternity.

Even when we are considering time as appertaining to the earth, it is not as simple as we may at first suppose. It does not always appear to be uniform. It can fly or drag according to our mood, yet if we try to prolong a particularly happy moment, we find this impossible. Conversely, moments in time can be stored in the memory and repeatedly enjoyed at leisure. The ageing process, also, is not constant, for the old can feel young within themselves and dance in spirit, despite the fact that their bodies are unable to do so.

More puzzling than this are the occasions when we seem able to make leaps forwards or backwards in time. Premonition and precognition are difficult to understand, but certainly happen. I, myself, have quite often been aware that I would meet someone, or have known just before they spoke what people would say. My sister and I have occasionally picked up each other's thoughts without any conscious effort or even intention, in fact this has usually happened when I have been very tired.

Our minds seem capable of making their own time rules. If we need to wake up at a certain hour, we usually find that we do so in advance of the alarm clock. Animals also possess this 'body clock'. Sometimes a dog will know exactly when his master is due home and will go to the gate to wait for him at the appropriate time.

Homing pigeons and migratory birds also appear to
have instincts which have developed far beyond our
own. They are probably guided by the natural laws of
time and space.

Time is a great deceiver. The young observe the
world about them, accept it as it is and expect it to
remain so. As we grow older we become aware that all
is imperceptibly changing. It is this very variation
which enriches life, broadens our outlook and provides
us with a wealth of experience. Although each day may
seem very much as the preceding one, this is never so. It
is not only that our bodies age, but when we look back
in history we see how each generation has differed
from the last in its morals, outlook and mode of life. In
the brief span of a human existence we are scarcely
aware of this onward movement. Evolution must
necessarily be very slow, but it continues inexorably;
deserts extend, rivers dry up or change course, rocks
are worn away, coastlines eroded, and once familiar
plant and animal species become extinct. Because this
progress is so gradual, we are almost as unconscious of
it as we are of the rotation of the earth. Yet the passage
of time is accomplishing so much. Just as the distance
between the stars seems too great for human imagining,
so we can scarcely visualise the length of time taken for
a chalk cliff or a coral reef to be formed from the build
up of the countless bodies of minute sea creatures that
comprise it. And if such vastness of time is incomprehensible to us, how much more so must be the notion of
eternity?

Eternity can only exist outside and independent of
planetary systems, which must, by their very nature,
include the passage of time. We have to escape from the
time concept altogether to be able to perceive it at all.
Once free of the limitations of time, and existing only
in a continuous 'present' state, it would, I think, then be

possible to enter again at will into any state of past or
future by returning to life within a planet such as our
own. There is no past or future, and therefore no time,
in eternity. Both Moses and Jesus spoke of God as "I
am".

Perhaps this experiencing of time is a necessary part
of our spiritual development. Life after death would, to
my mind, be of little worth if it offered merely a
perpetual slothful existence in boundless pleasure
gardens. Even the saintliest of us is far from attaining a
state of perfection at the close of an earthly life. It
seems reasonable to suppose that, hereafter, we shall
continue on our pre-ordained pilgrimage. We gain
valuable knowledge here on earth, but obviously we
still have so much more to learn and understand. In
eternity, surely, the progression must continue.

We can best understand time and eternity, perhaps,
when we see them, not as contradictory states, but as
one complete entity. Blake believed that it was possible
to "hold Infinity in the palm of your hand, and Eternity
in an hour".

Sometimes the two seem to run parallel to each
other; our bodies and minds maturing and ageing on
earth, while our true selves are developing in eternity.
Eternity cannot be a line which we move along; rather
it is a state of continuous harmony, joy and peace,
which may be entered or left at will, so that we exist
either in time or eternity, or perhaps in both at the
same point.

It is difficult to imagine how time would be viewed
from eternity. We see the world through the limitations
of human eyes and bodies. Were we to experience it
without such impediments, it would surely present a
far more wonderful aspect. What unknown colours
may stretch beyond the spectrum; what unimagined
sounds outside our aural register? So much beauty

remains hidden from us, and if it were possible to roam at will unhampered by the vulnerability of the human body, without weariness, hunger, pain or fear, this would be an experience akin to heaven.

When we seek to view the world from some position outside it, we begin to catch a glimpse of life in its fullest sense. We see the evolutionary process as a continuing one, the venturing of man into space as a step comparable to, and having as far-reaching consequences as, the emergence of marine life on to dry land. Stage follows stage; nothing is random and nothing is lost. When we think we have begun to see and understand God's plan, we come upon yet a greater stage beyond it, and then another beyond that. Wonder succeeds wonder, and human minds cannot conceive the extent of creation. We can only marvel at its magnitude.

Time has been pictured as a river, "an ever-rolling stream", and this is a most fitting metaphor. The water in a stream is in constant motion, yet the stream itself presents the same appearance as the years pass by. If we examine it closely, however, we see that it is, nonetheless, continually changing. A leaf floats by and is sucked into a swirling eddy, fish rise to the surface or dart among the shallows, sunlight sparkles across its ripples, or heavy rain causes it to rise to a higher level. These may be seen as events crossing the surface of time. Events come and go: time continues. Yet even the river is limited in its own existence, as is time. A planet's life is not for ever; it will eventually change or disintegrate. It seems likely, though, that out of all death new birth will arise. Our sun may in some way regenerate itself, as seeds renew the life of a plant. Time, then, will continue to be, but timelessness remains with God alone.

John Donne saw heaven as having "no ends nor

beginnings, but one equal eternity", but of all the visions of eternity I find the clearest to be that portrayed by Henry Vaughan:

I saw Eternity the other night
Like a great ring of pure and endless light,
All calm as it was bright.
And round beneath it, Time, in hours, days, years,
Driven by the spheres,
Like a vast shadow moved – in which the world
And all her train were hurled.

Here, again, is the idea of eternity as a circle, but not a moving circle. He sees it as still, utterly beautiful and peaceful, in complete contrast to the shadowy time, which is in continuous and turbulent motion. This, I think, is the nearest we can come to imagining these two states of being. I have sometimes thought that eternity is being built up out of the bricks of time, both states being inextricably interwoven; thus it may be that by living through time we are able to gain eternity.

10. Wisdom and Folly

What is wisdom? I suppose the simplest definition is that it is a right understanding of truth; being able to discern which things in life are important and which trivial. It has little to do with the accumulation of knowledge, for the simplest of souls may be wise and the most learned pursue false trails. Getting our priorities right is essential if we are to live fulfilled and happy lives, yet we so often give little thought to this, being content to drift purposelessly through our days.

The Bible lays great emphasis on the value of wisdom. The psalms and proverbs stress it over and over again – "the fear of the Lord is the beginning of wisdom", "wisdom is the principal thing", "incline thine ear unto wisdom", and so on. In Ecclesiastes we are told that "wisdom giveth life" and Job declared "the price of wisdom is above rubies". From the seers, prophets and soothsayers of the Old Testament to the Magi in the New we see this continuing search for truth, which in the Bible is synonymous with God.

The possession of wisdom is not a human achievement but a gift from God. Solomon, renowned for his great wisdom, prayed at the beginning of his reign not for power and wealth but that he might have wisdom and knowledge to understand the hearts of those over whom he would rule. It was granted to him in such abundance that, many years later, the Queen of Sheba proclaimed, "Behold the one half of the greatness of thy wisdom was not told me: for thou exceedest the fame that I heard. Happy are thy men, and happy are these thy servants, which stand continually before thee and hear thy wisdom".

But the ways of man are so often far from the ways of God. Frequently that which appears to be wise in our sight is foolishness in the light of truth. Our values, our standards, not only fall short, but are sometimes quite contrary to God's. St. Paul declared, "The wisdom of this world is foolishness with God. The Lord knoweth the thoughts of the wise, that they are vain. Hath not God made foolish the wisdom of this world?" Man, throughout history, has amassed stores of knowledge; he has delved far below the earth's crust, reached to the moon, travelled into the remotest corners of his planet, studied science, mathematics and language, learned to control disease and, through psychoanalysis, to better understand his fellow man. But he has only to look out into the vastness of the universe to know that the whole sum of his knowledge is as a speck of dust in comparison with all that is as yet undiscovered and beyond his ken. Homo sapiens he may be, but he is far from possessing all wisdom.

It is so easy to mistake folly for wisdom and to aspire to unworthy aims and standards. The cynic may sincerely believe that "most friendship is feigning, most loving mere folly". We all set ourselves an aim in life. It may be to follow a chosen career, to marry and have children, to gain fame or wealth, to travel the world or to acquire power and influence over others.

We need to be certain that the path we seek to follow is the right one and the goal it leads to worthy of attaining. "What shall it profit a man", asked Jesus, "if he shall gain the whole world, and lose his own soul?"

Sometimes, however, actions which appear to be foolish are, in effect, quite the reverse. The bird that lights to earth just in front of a prowling stoat, dragging one wing along the ground as if injured, is not being foolhardy but is luring the predator away from her nest hidden in the grasses.

A story is told of the "wise fools of Gotham". In the days of King John the villagers heard that the king and his retinue intended to visit them. Entertaining the monarch could prove ruinous to a small community, so they set out to demonstrate that they were unworthy of his patronage. They were discovered attempting to drown an eel in the village pond, rolling cheeses down a hill in order that they would go to market on their own accord, building a shelter to protect the trees in a wood from the hot sun and erecting a fence round a bush on which a cuckoo had settled so that the bird would not be able to fly away. The king contemptuously decided to bypass a village which housed such idiots, so their supposed foolishness had secured their purpose and, in their case, was certainly wisdom.

The position of a jester, or fool, in the court of a mediaeval king was a curious one. Ostensibly his function was merely to amuse and divert the monarch, yet frequently he would become the king's most trusted adviser. Unlike so many of his fellow courtiers, who used insincere flattery in order to curry favour and would try to discredit each other in pursuit of their own advancement, the jester had no particular axe to grind and could declare his mind honestly. Consequently, it was often the fool who spoke with wisdom and whose counsel was relied on by the king. We find evidence of this in some of Shakespeare's plays.

In the Bible we are told that a simple and child-like mind is able more readily than an apparently learned one to understand the mysteries of God.

How, then, can true wisdom be obtained and how distinguished from mere folly?

"Go to the ant, thou sluggard.

Consider her ways and be wise", says the old proverb.

Certainly we must work to find understanding; it does not drop into our laps unsought. Yet it is far more than a gathering together of facts. We have to be able to interpret those facts, assess their value and so discern truth and worth from falsehood and dross. Wisdom may also include prudence and forethought, as in the story of the wise and foolish virgins. The treasures of wisdom are hidden, yet not so deeply but that they may be uncovered if we are prepared to take the trouble to search for them. Like the gold and jewels in the tomb of an Ancient Egyptian king, lying unsuspected beneath the desert sand for centuries, they are there, waiting for their beauty to be revealed.

Perhaps wisdom may often be confused with folly and one mistaken for the other, but in the final analysis the only real wisdom must be a knowledge of what is truth, and therefore a knowledge of God Himself. There can be no greater wisdom than this.

11. Sound and Silence

There is a book written by Elizabeth Goudge which has as its title, "The Scent of Water". This would, at first, appear to be ludicrous since water is odourless. However, on consideration, we realise that it is indeed possible to detect the presence of water at a distance. Wild creatures can certainly do so, for the quality and humidity of the atmosphere is changed and they are sensitive to this. Plants and trees growing near a stream will give out their own freshness which we are aware of as we approach them.

It would, thus, in a similar way, be possible to speak of "the sound of silence", for silence, to my mind, is not merely an absence of sound, but has a definite quality of its own and exudes its beneficial properties in the same way as a stream of flowing water.

Inanimate and silent objects which possess no power of speech can yet convey thoughts and impressions to our minds. Shakespeare wrote of "tongues in trees" and "sermons in stones". We read in the psalms, "The heavens declare the glory of God. Day unto day uttereth speech and night unto night showeth knowledge. There is no speech or language where their voice is not heard..." We need, perhaps, an alternative to speech to understand the voice of silence. The key may be in the lines of the hymn:

> ... the silence of Eternity
> Interpreted by love.

In silence there can be an intimacy of companionship which is totally absent when sounds intrude. Many friends of long standing or married couples experience this; they know each other's thoughts so well and their minds are so attuned that words are unnecessary and they can sit or walk together contentedly with silence as a bond between them. The well-known words of the Desiderata advise, "Go placidly amid the noise and haste and remember what peace there may be in silence".

Sound, however, is the normal way of communication between living creatures of any species. It is best achieved through some sort of language and, through the ages, this has developed and become increasingly refined in man to allow for subtle nuances of thought which can be expressed in eloquent poetry or fine prose. The lower animals and birds also use sound to a greater or lesser extent to signal to each other, but also employ body movements, especially in courtship or to indicate hostility. In man this, too, does play a part, but to a much smaller degree.

It does seem as if words are necessary as vehicles of thought. It is, of course, possible to survive without the need for very deep thought, using natural instincts to avoid danger, and concentrating only on obtaining sufficient food and shelter and a partner in order to satisfy the basic needs of life, but this is only existing on an animal level. Man's brain has developed to allow him to live on a higher plane than this; to seek to understand the mysteries of the universe, to look back to his origins and forward to his destiny, to discover beauty and to seek to create it for himself in art, poetry, literature and music, to be able to reason logically and so enter the realms of mathematics, physics, science and astronomy. To do this he has needed language, both for the ordered construction of his own thoughts and in order to communicate these thoughts to others. The conveyance of thought may be either written or spoken, but language is necessary for both, and the extent of vocabulary available will govern the depth to which that thought may be expressed.

When our thoughts reach out to a more exalted level, and we attempt to become attuned to God and to communicate with Him, we naturally need language to work out theology, to record man's past experiences in his search for life's meaning and, in our worship, we make use of our finest poetry and music to express our need of God and our adoration of Him.

Yet we frequently find that we come closer to God not through sound, however beautiful, but in silence. The monks of old knew the value of this and set aside part of each day for quiet meditation. In our busy twentieth century world this is an almost forgotten art and we are having to re-learn how to rest our minds in silent contemplation. Some have discovered it through studying Eastern religions, or practising Yoga, but we do not need to travel so far afield; it is here at the heart of Christianity. The Quakers have a saying, "True silence is to the spirit as sleep is to the body; a source of nourishment and refreshment".

It is so easy to spend our times of prayer continuously speaking as we pour out our own needs and desires, but allowing no space for God's words to reach us. It is as necessary in any conversation to listen as to speak, perhaps even more so. The familiar Bible stories reveal that God's word could only be heard by those who were prepared to listen. His is the 'still, small voice', so easy to overlook amid the noise and clamour of our busy lives; all too readily dismissed as something trivial and of no account. God, as the psalmist knew, is everywhere present, in the heights, in the depths and in the uttermost parts of the earth, yet it is possible to live our lives completely oblivious of Him. Everything that is of worth must be sought for, and to hear the voice of God will need our very utmost attention and diligence. He will come to us in the silence of our hearts when we have tuned our minds to be receptive to His voice and can shut out all alien sound.

Nevertheless, the sounds of the earth are of great value and beauty. Those who are born deaf miss so much that is of inestimable worth; the wind in the trees, birdsong in all its variation, the murmuring of streams over rocks or surf breaking on the shore, the faint calls of animals and the hum of insect life which drift to our ears as we walk through the countryside; even the mingled sounds of the city can be pleasant background, and certainly the voices of friends and loved ones can bring great delight. Yet, there are also times when sound can cease to have meaning, when it jars and obtrudes on our senses and becomes merely noise. Incessant chatter about trivial matters can grow utterly boring, and if we are exposed to noise such as that made by a pneumatic drill or loud machinery for any length of time we long for silence. A mother of a constantly crying baby finds herself exhausted by the strain. Excessive noise can, indeed, be damaging to our hearing and a cause of stress.

Some people, on the other hand, fear silence and dislike being alone in an empty house. If this is unavoidable they will turn on the television or radio in order to have a background of some kind of sound.

This, I think, is unwise, for to give ourselves no time to be alone with our thoughts will surely impoverish our minds and narrow the development of our lives.

Speech can be eloquent and can enrich us beyond measure, yet foolish or meaningless chatter can have the opposite effect. It is not necesary when we pray, said Jesus, to use "vain repetitions". Our prayers are not made more effective because of our "much speaking". Some religions believe that they are, and chants and incantations are repeated over and over again. Words alone, without the thought behind them can only be meaningless. They have no mysterious powers in themselves.

Just as colours may exist beyond the spectrum seen by our eyes, so there will be sounds of higher and lower frequency than our ears are capable of registering. We know that some animals hear these. We cannot always reproduce sounds by using a musical scale; for instance, it would be impossible to play or to sing exactly the notes made by a flowing stream, and birdsong is extremely difficult to imitate. However, broadly speaking, I suppose that sound in its most perfect form can be described as music. The word 'music' implies pleasure to us and also brings with it the essence of silence. It speaks to the heart as well as to the ear. Donne perceived this when, in a vision of heaven, he described it as the place where there would be, " . . . no noise nor silence, but one equal music".

I do not believe sound and silence to be in opposition. Silence is not the negation of sound, since silence has its own voice; just as sound which deteriorates into noise can become a kind of silence for it has no meaningful language. Thus we may have the sound of silence and also the silence of sound. Perhaps we should seek to translate both into true music, and thus discover Donne's definition of heaven.

12. Chance and Destiny

It is very difficult to determine how much that makes up life comes about by pure chance and how much is pre-determined. We awake to a new morning and we plan the day ahead, yet we can only foresee a broad outline of what will actually take place. The phone may ring, an acquaintance stop us in the street, we may witness a traffic accident, feel uplifted by the sight of a carpet of bluebells under the trees, find that the milkman has failed to call or that the boiler is not working. Hundreds of unpredictable incidents such as these will make up a single day, and most of us, on returning home in the evening, will enjoy recounting its pleasures and pains to the family.

When we look back on life we can often see that the course of events has frequently been completely turned by some apparently trivial occurrence. Quite fortuitously we may meet the man or woman we will marry, some slight error or oversight is enough to cause a serious accident bringing about injury or death, the delay of only a few minutes can result in the loss of an important job, or, on the other hand, may save us from being involved in some dangerous situation. As the rhyme reminds us:

> For the want of a nail the shoe was lost,
> For the want of a shoe the horse was lost,
> For the want of a horse the rider was lost,
> For the want of the rider the battle was lost,
> For the want of the battle the nation was lost
> And all for the want of a horseshoe nail.

So much seems to hang on chance. To what extent are we simply the victims of a haphazard whirl of circumstance? Not, I think, entirely. We have a great deal of responsibility for the course of our own lives, and it is my belief that we are guided in certain directions if we are willing thus to be led. Yet in no way are we forced along pre-ordained paths. At all stages of our lives we are at liberty to change direction if we so wish.

Despite the fact that pure chance does exist, there appears to be a certain law of averages so that, to some extent, we can determine the likelihood of an event occurring. In throwing a dice we can be sure that eventually a six will appear. Gamblers are well aware of the odds involved. It is far more risky to gamble on a roulette game than it is on horse or dog racing where some skill or judgement may be employed in assessing the most likely winner.

Certainty is not assured, of course, but a measure of probability may be worked out. Forecasting the weather, for example, is a skill which makes use of known previous weather patterns, observation of cloud formation and wind direction over a wide area, and the scientific knowledge of climatic changes. Thus, though the weather is constantly changing apparently at random, a degree of accuracy may be expected in predicting conditions for the near future.

In the past, however, many religions believed that man's destiny was in the hands of the gods, and that the Fates, Nemesis, or the stars were in entire control of his being. There are some today who will make no effort to improve their lot or attempt to escape from adverse circumstances because they believe that all to befall them is the will of Allah and cannot be changed. According to the Greeks, Nemesis apportioned good or evil fortune to mankind, while the Fates, three sisters, were in charge of the thread of mortal life. To Clotho was entrusted its spinning, Lachesis measured its length, and Atropos slit the fragile thread when its appointed time had run. Man was completely at their mercy.

There were many ancient ways of predicting the future. Prophets or seers were held in veneration and often spoke through visions or dreams. In Greece, it was customary to consult the oracle which involved visiting a special temple where the priestess, or sibyl, would make her usually obscure pronouncements. The Romans sometimes went through a ritual whereby a soothsayer would arrange the entrails of a dead animal and thus divine hidden truths. Witchdoctors in Africa used bones to help them determine a person guilty of some crime. Most common of all practices was the drawing of lots. This is mentioned many times in the Bible, for instance in discovering Jonah's responsibility for the storm, and as employed by the Roman soldiers at the time of the Crucifixion.

Even in Christianity there was once a school of thought which believed in pre-destination. Some at birth were allocated to be saved; others condemned to hell. Only a favoured few were thought to have been set aside by God as His chosen people. I cannot see how this could ever be justified by Biblical teaching since, from Genesis onwards, man has been given a free choice between good and evil and, should he stray from the right path, is told continually that if he repents and returns he is assured of God's forgiveness. In Victorian times, some people opposed reform laws to benefit the poor, maintaining that God appoints us to our appropriate station in life. In the words of the hymn, now usually omitted:

> The rich man in his castle
> The poor man at his gate,
> God made them high and lowly
> And ordered their estate.

The caste system in India is another example of this.

Today there still exists widespread belief in some kind of pre-ordination in our lives. Many confide implicitly in the influence of the stars and eagerly study their horoscopes, while others will consult fortune tellers. Superstitions of all kinds abound and, although most people deny taking them seriously, it is noticeable that most of us will avoid walking under a ladder, and that estate agents frequently find it difficult to sell a house that is numbered 13. I find superstitions very interesting, and it is often fascinating to discover their origins. Quite a number are relics of pre-Christian ceremonies. My mother, who was country-born, taught us much of the old country folk-lore when we were children, and a great deal of it is based on observation of the land and respect for its plant and animal life. Were we, however, to take seriously all the common superstitions and prohibitions life would become almost impossible, for we should be constantly performing rituals to ward off evil and seeking to escape potential producers of ill-fortune. In one of George Borrow's books he describes a man so obsessed.

When we speak of good or bad luck we imply that somehow fortune is being decided for us. Luck of either kind is not dependent on any sort of effort by us. We may say that a person is lucky to be born into a rich family, to win a large prize in a competition, or to enjoy good health. Luck in that sense certainly exists, but in most cases success in life depends on hard work and determination and the use of one's own abilities.

We sometimes feel that we can make things happen by thinking along certain lines. We may suppose that if we worry enough in advance of some dreaded possibility we can prevent it from happening. Usually this is a forlorn hope, though it is true that things never seem to occur exactly as we have anticipated. We may even try to bargain with God and say, for example, "If I recover from this illness I will live a better life," (or give money to this or that cause, or give up some bad habit, or whatever the case may be). It seems rather a childish belief to suppose that we can enter into such negotiations with God. If He were to reward us according to our actions, I fear that most of us would fare badly, and it is indeed fortunate that, "He maketh His sun to rise on the evil and on the good, and sendeth rain on the just and on the unjust".

But what of prayer? Surely this is able to change the natural course of events. Is it not true that much in life is not blind chance at all but that, 'all things are working together for good'? I believe so, but the important thing to remember is that God does not employ a kind of magic, manipulating us as mindless puppets to do His will. He works in co-operation with us, and prayer is a force involving both God and man. I consider it to be a very powerful force, and that through it God is able to bring about all that is good and desirable on earth. I am sure that for each one of us there is a specific task to fulfil; a right path to travel during our life span. I think that we are all equipped with the necessary character-istics to achieve that potential, regardless of adverse circumstances which may surround us, just as a ship can set its sails and travel in any direction, despite contrary winds. A daisy cannot develop into a buttercup, nor can we live our lives as carbon copies of others. We should aim to make the best possible use of the particular talents entrusted to us, and we can certainly look to God for help and guidance.

Prayer is the means we have of linking our wills to His. It is, perhaps, as Blake said, like a golden thread:

> I give you the end of a golden string,
> Only wind it into a ball.
> It will lead you in at Heaven's gate
> Built in Jerusalem's wall.

So, in my view, life is neither governed by blind chance nor pre-destined for us. We have the responsibility of choosing the route we will take, but we also have God's guidance if we will accept it, so that we need have no fear of losing the way. However hard the going may be, we can 'go out into the darkness and put our hand into the hand of God'.

13. Natural and Supernatural

By natural we usually mean something which happens in a predictable way within the range of our experience, or that is independent of any manipulation by man. We describe as supernatural anything which appears to be contrary to the laws of nature as we know them, anything relating to God, or a mysterious happening for which we can find no logical explanation. We cannot be too precise in these definitions, however. We can only bring a limited knowledge and experience of the working of the universe to bear on the question of whether an event is supernatural, or merely an as yet undiscovered scientific truth. Primitive man would have regarded the power of electricity and gas as miraculous; an earthquake, thunder, and the eruption of a volcano were taken by him as signs of the gods' displeasure.

There are some natural events, such as eclipses or the appearance of a comet, which occur only rarely. Nowadays, these can be predicted easily enough by scientists, but they would have terrified our ancestors because they were outside their everyday experience of life. Thus it may be that our descendants will find scientific and logical explanations for many aspects of life which perplex us today.

A great deal of our existence is puzzling and bewildering. It is possible, of course, to live our lives completely on a materialistic level, working only in order to obtain sufficient wealth to provide us with the maximum of pleasure and happiness. Life, however, so often frustrates this. We find ourselves coping with illness and loss, disappointment and frustration, old-age and death. We rebel against the injustice of it all asking, 'Why?', 'What is the point of anything?' And it is when we start to try to find a meaning to life that we turn to the supernatural. It is becoming fashionable in our present time to delve into the preternatural and the occult. It is as if we are searching but do not know which way to turn. Some are seeking truths from the well-established religions of the world; others are trying to discover new cults which will provide them with a purposeful reason for living. There is a great dissatisfaction in human minds which, however materialistic we become, seems to pull us back into the quest for God. As St. Augustine said, "Thou hast made us for Thyself, and our souls are restless until we rest in Thee".

Is all that is supernatural good and appertaining to God, though? What of the forces of evil? Many religions warn of evil spirits and their power over human minds. I think that we need to exercise care. Just as both fire and water which are vital to life can, if misused, destroy it, so we should avoid venturing into areas which we cannot as yet fully understand. I have always thought that spiritualism should be treated warily, though I am quite sure that good is greater than evil and that if we turn towards God we are protected from anything which may be spiritually harmful. Our own wills are vitally important. If we wish for and seek goodness and truth we shall eventually discover it.

A supernatural event is often described as a miracle and, again, we need to look carefully at what exactly we mean by miraculous. I think that, like prayer, a true miracle is brought about when the power of God works in combination with the faith of man. Time and again, in the healing miracles of Jesus, we read how faith was required of the sick person, or in certain cases, the faith of someone else on his behalf. We are also told that sometimes no miracles were possible because of the people's unbelief. We cannot really explain a miracle, because it seems to happen contrary to the normal way of nature, but I think it true to say that mind can influence matter in certain circumstances.

Doctors are sometimes baffled when a progressive disease is inexplicably halted; we read of people walking through fire unscathed, or lying on nails without being injured. These are not normal occurrences, however, and cannot be carried out as a matter of course. It seems that power both from within and without the person concerned must somehow merge, and most miracles involve a use of our bodies in some way. Thus, if such a power is dormant in us, we cannot say that something impossible has been done when a miracle takes place. It is, rather, something which we are unable to understand. I do not, though, think that God ever suspends or alters a law which is solely natural and has no relation to man. For instance, the story in the book of Joshua about the sun and the moon remaining still in the sky for a whole day cannot, surely, be taken literally, nor the account of the shadow on Hezekiah's sundial going backwards by ten degrees.

There has always been much speculation as to whether God's power is limitless. It must be so, in my opinion. Yet I have heard questions posed which seem to me similar to the kind the Pharisees and Sadducees put to Jesus in an attempt to discredit His teaching. One such is, "Can God make a stone so heavy that He cannot lift it?" It is on a level with the well-known "Have you stopped beating your wife?" poser. Neither 'yes' nor 'no' would be the correct answer. I would say, though, that if the question about God is to be taken seriously, the answer MUST be 'no'; but obviously it is a faulty question, since it presumes that God has the limitations of man. Just as obviously, we would say that although God is omnipotent He cannot, by His very nature, commit an evil act or nullify His existence.

Over the years the subject of angels has been much discussed. Are they a separate order of beings or, perhaps, manifestations of God's presence in a way which we are more easily able to comprehend? From Biblical accounts both seem possible, and with a limited human understanding, we can only dimly grasp what is meant by an angelic vision. Certainly we hear of the angel of God's presence, or it may be that because we live on earth, and therefore have our existence within the confines of time, our angelic counterpart is co-existing in eternity. This, perhaps, would explain the words of Jesus when He warned, "Take heed that ye despise not one of these little ones, for I say unto you that in heaven their angels do always behold the face of my Father which is in heaven".

Most people in discussing the supernatural will refer to ghosts, though it is difficult to determine just what is meant by this term. Because much folk lore and superstition has built up over the years, ghosts are usually feared, and a reputation for being haunted is sufficient to prevent a house from being sold. Yet ghosts are reputed merely to be the spirits of the dead and, if we did not fear them living, why should they assume malevolent powers after death? I feel that this is, again, an area where, because we have so little certain knowledge, we have built up a great deal of fantasy, and it is not easy to distinguish truth from fiction. I think it very probable that most ghostly manifestations are brought about by strong emotions felt during a person's lifetime, which have remained within the walls of a house where they can be 'picked up' by anyone who is sensitive to the atmosphere of that particular place. Some people are extremely intuitive in this way. Many ancient buildings seem to hold echoes from the past, just as churches, particularly old ones, retain an impression of calm and prayer. I lived once in a reputedly haunted house and it did indeed hold a strange atmosphere of its own but, far from this being frightening, I always felt safe and protected there.

In recent years scientific advance has made us speculate on the possibility of life on other planets or in galaxies beyond our own. Such is surely possible and, were we to be visited by beings from outer space, we could scarcely regard them as supernatural creatures, since they would be as much a part of the universe as ourselves.

Primitive man must have found so much that was beyond his understanding that it is scarcely surprising that he lived in a state of fear. To him, the gods were unpredictable and must be appeased and placated by gifts and sacrifice. As scientific progress advances and we begin, however dimly, to understand more of the universe about us, our wonder grows at its sheer immensity and complexity. We can comprehend only the tiniest fraction of creation, but as knowledge grows, much that we had thought supernatural is explained to us. Were we to possess, eventually, absolute wisdom and perception, it might be that natural and supernatural would merge into one Utopian perfection.

14. Give and Take

The words give and take conjure up memories of arithmetic lessons at school when we learned the principles of adding and subtracting. To subtract was the negative action, and to take away always meant to diminish the original number until, when our arithmetical knowledge became more advanced, we understood that to take away a minus quantity was, in effect, an addition. This more complex concept is true of the giving and taking which makes up everyday life. Taking can be a positive action, for we can take a walk, take heart, take sides etc; while giving may often be negative as when we give up, or give ground.

The whole of life, indeed, is made up of an exchange between these two aspects and, almost always, the practice of one will involve the other. When the tide goes out and recedes from one shore, it will, at the same time, be encroaching on the opposite one. That giving and taking are interchangeable is recognised by St. Francis in the well-known prayer where he concludes,

for it is in giving that we receive,
it is in pardoning that we are pardoned,
and it is in dying that we are born to eternal life.

When we are young the virtues of generosity and
unselfishness are impressed upon us. A small child
instinctively desires to take, and this is a natural
reaction to ensure survival. The fledgling in the nest
clamours incessantly to be fed. However, when
babyhood is outgrown, a child must learn to share his
sweets and treasured possessions. At first he will be
most unwilling to do so, until he finds that it is not all
sacrifice on his part alone, for he too will receive
consideration and co-operation from his fellows. 'It is',
we are taught, 'more blessed to give than to receive.'
Children discover that much pleasure is involved in the
making and offering of presents to those they love.

It is usually much later in life that we learn that there
can also be virtue in receiving. It is not always easy to
feel sincere gratitude and sometimes we resent others'
gifts, feeling that we are being patronised or made the
objects of charity. To receive graciously, to be able to
please the giver by accepting with love, is sometimes
harder than the act of giving. Each requires a spirit of
generosity. Most parents understand this well and will
appreciate a shabby, home-made card over which a
small child has toiled, far more than an expensive
bought one on which no effort has been expended. My
mother treasured all her life a most hideous glass vase,
bright orange in colour, which my sister and I had
pooled our pocket money to purchase from Woolworths
for her one Christmas. We had given much earnest
thought to its choice and, in our eyes, it was the most
desirable object in the store, so she, too, saw it as
beautiful, because it expressed our love for her.

Another lesson to be learned about giving is that

whatever we give is returned to us in some way. "Cast thy bread upon the waters", says the Bible, "for thou shalt find it after many days". "Give and it shall be given unto you". It is rather like playing tennis. We send the ball over the net and it is immediately returned. A more modern saying points out that we cannot spray perfume on others without a few drops falling on ourselves, and we realise the truth of the song which declares,

> I want to be happy
> But I can't be happy
> Till I've made you happy too.

If, then, we endeavour to put good into life, we shall eventually receive back that which is also good.

On the other hand, we can, if we so choose, live only for what we gain from life; we can try to take out of it that which rightly belongs to others, we can refuse to contribute anything of our own and, for a while, we may appear to prosper. But, sooner or later we shall find that all we have gained has become worthless dross, just as a miser may die friendless and unloved, finding little comfort from his accumulated gold. We have to make a positive donation to the world we live in for,

> life without purpose is barren indeed;
> you can't have a harvest unless you sow seed.

The world does not owe us a living; happiness is not ours by right.

It is even possible to err by going to the other extreme and attempting to live without ever taking. Those who feel that all pleasure is sinful; that it is wicked to sing, dance, listen to music, laugh and take time to relax and enjoy the beauty of the earth, are spurning the blessings which God freely bestows upon us. Those who decline to take any gifts or repayments and insist on being completely independent and self sufficient become unlovable, for love must involve mutual giving. Jesus condemned those who, like the Pharisees, would give, not out of love, but in order that their generosity might impress others. We are in receipt of countless precious gifts; our very being, our health and strength, our ability to see, hear, touch, taste, the whole miracle of life and the wonder of our universe; with all these we are endowed at birth.

> I learned it on the meadow path,
> I learned it on the mountain stairs,
> The best things any mortal has
> Are those which every mortal shares.

So we are told, "Freely ye have received, freely give," and sharing with one another is, surely, the most reasonable way for us to live.

When we consider nature we are aware of this balance between giving and taking. The existence of one species is dependent upon another. Air and water are purified by plant life for plants take in the waste carbon dioxide breathed out by animals. A seed falls into the earth and dies in order that a new plant may have its birth. We love each other because love begets love. When we become aware of the extent of God's love for us, we are drawn to Him in return. "We love Him because He first loved us." And this same taking and giving which we see throughout life, is there in death also. In the words of the hymn,

> I lay in dust, life's glory dead,
> And from the ground there blossoms red
> Life that shall endless be.

15. Hope and Despair

Here are two of the most frequently felt emotions, for most of our lives we will veer between these states. Whether by nature we are optimists or pessimists, most of us expect some pleasure to await us in the future. "Hope", said Pope, "springs eternal in the human breast. Man never is, but always to be blest."

Naturally, when our expectations are frustrated we become disillusioned and disappointed, though we will not experience utter despair until every vestige of hope has been finally abandoned. It is, therefore, reasonable to assume that of the two hope will predominate. Even the most traumatic experience need not completely extinguish it. Our own natures will determine the extent to which both qualities fill our minds; the degree of suffering or loss is disproportionate. Some can remain cheerful and contented in the face of tremendous odds against them, while others will give up at the first breath of misfortune.

Despair is always a personal decision. It is a letting go of the rope to which we have been clinging. The rope itself is never withdrawn from us; hope is an enduring quality, but it may require of us much patience, fortitude and determination if we are to retain our grip on it.

The story is told of two men who were lost overboard from a ship during the hours of darkness. No-one saw the accident and the ship steamed on leaving them alone in a waste of waters. They swam and floated throughout the night and, when daylight came, realised the extent of their plight, far off the busy shipping routes, mere specks in the boundless ocean. One gave up, allowing himself to sink and drown, but the other, hopeless though it seemed, kept on swimming. Later that day a helicopter which had been sent out to search for them reached the area and, against all probability, the man was sighted and rescued.

Despair is to believe that something is entirely unattainable and to write it off. This does not mean that it actually IS impossible, however much it may seem so. "You cannot tie water in a lump", says an African proverb. But if it became ice this could be achieved with ease. When I was at school we were taught that an atom was the smallest possible particle, incapable of being divided. Before 1939 it was a common belief that Britain could not survive a second world war. History has disproved both of these suppositions. Despair, too, can be transformed into hope. To hope in the face of whatever may befall does not come easily, though, and fortunate indeed is the man who can say,

> I laugh for hope has happy place with me,
> If my barque sinks, 'tis to another sea.

To all of us, even the most optimistic, there will come times when our spirits are low. This is to be expected and we need to remember, as the old Desiderata reminds us, that "many fears are born of fatigue and loneliness".

Of course, just as despair may be needless, there can also be false hopes. Neither word conveys absolute certainty in the eventual outcome. Hope must contain some element of doubt; if it did not, it would be certitude. Equally, if we see despair as hope lost, then it is possible that it may still be retrieved. Sometimes it seems that hope grows best from adversity, just as flowers will so often flourish in poor soil, while those planted in more fertile earth will produce mainly leaves. As Shelley said:

> Our sincerest laughter,
> With some pain is fraught;
> Our sweetest songs are those that tell of
>   saddest thought.

Sorrow and affliction need not produce despair. They frequently bring out our better qualities of courage, patience and endurance; even a strengthening of hope.

A popular hymn speaks of the uncertainty and confusion on a battlefield, where amid the noise and distractions it is difficult to know which side is gaining ground and whether there is cause for hope or despair.

> If hopes were dupes, fears may be liars.
> It may be, in yon smoke concealed,
> Your comrades chase e'en now the fliers,
> And, but for you, possess the field.

It is obvious that we should aim to preserve a hopeful outlook; to look for the best in others will usually result in our finding it. If we go through life anticipating doom and disaster, we can all too often bring these very things upon us. To profess an utterly despairing philosophy is to deny the possibility of anything unexpected, unpredicted or, indeed, miraculous. Although some of us are, by nature, more cheerful than others, we can to some extent control our attitude to life. It seems to me wise to steer a middle course, neither throwing all caution to the winds, like the man who refuses to insure his house because he supposes that fire or burglary could never happen to him, nor to be so fearful of calamity that we refuse to travel by car or plane lest we should be involved in an accident. How wise is the old proverb, "Hope for the best, but prepare for the worst".

Hope and despair appear to deny each other, yet obviously both exist. It is precisely because we have hoped that we despair, then out of that despair hope returns when we least expect it. This we see most clearly in the resurrection of Jesus. Hope ends in realisation, and throughout life goes on renewing itself, reaching ever onwards; otherwise existence would be meaningless.

My own belief is that, not only is hope available as our constant companion throughout life, but that even out of the darkest and most despairing situation that same hope will be reborn. Despair is capable of being transformed into hope. The blacker the night, the more beautiful the dawn.

There is no pity in the endless sea,
No feeling in the waves that tear and tear;
But wrestle, vainly striving for the air,
Not yet despair;
Enduring for the hope that still may be.

Scornful, contemptuous, every wave comes down;
Fierce, colourless, with bitter, cruel blow,
Each stronger than the last, in power they grow;
Down, down below
To thrust us deep and triumph as we drown.

Futile to struggle, helpless and alone;
Feeling is numb and all desire has fled;
Sink then, and let the waves flow overhead,
No tear to shed,
Death will but quench the anguish we have known.

Let go: yet has the evil now increased;
There is no light, no hope; on every side
The fiends of darkness gather and deride;
No place to hide,
And all the pain of loneliness released.

But sinking, when resistance is no more,
Drawn by deep currents stronger than the tide,
Hindered no longer by our stubborn pride,
The storms subside
And quiet waters bring us to the shore.

A shore well-known; yet altered to our sight.
Black clouds that on the midnight sky hung low
Enhance the dawning with a roseate glow
And daybreak know,
When darkness scatters in the path of light.

Is it not so? Out of our deepest pain
New life is born; and surely it shall be
In the pure radiance of eternity
Our destiny
To tread through darkness to the dawn again.

16. Joy and Sorrow

Almost all that is true of hope and despair applies equally to our experience of joy and sorrow. Both are intrinsically woven into life and, just as hope can grow out of despair, so sorrow can be turned into joy. It is as if happiness must be spun from the thread of suffering. There is a saying, "The woof of life is dark, but it is shot with a warp of gold". Blake expressed the same thought:

> Joy and woe are woven fine
> A clothing for the soul divine;
> Under every grief and pine
> Runs a joy with silken twine.

The psalms tell us that pain and suffering may be our lot, but although "weeping may endure for a night, joy cometh in the morning". "They that sow in tears shall reap in joy".

Kahlil Gibran amplifies this concept more fully, and his words will sum up far better than I all that could be written on the subject in this chapter:

"Then a woman said, 'Speak to us of Joy and Sorrow',
and he answered:
'Your joy is your sorrow unmasked,
and the selfsame well from which your laughter rises
was oftentimes filled with your tears.
And how else can it be?
The deeper that sorrow carves into your being
the more joy you can contain. Is not the cup that
holds your wine the very cup that was burned in the
                                        potter's oven,
and is not the lute that soothes your spirit
the very wood that was hollowed with knives?
When you are joyous, look deep into your heart
and you will find it is only that which
has given you sorrow that is giving you joy.
When you are sorrowful, look again in your heart,
and you shall see that, in truth, you are weeping
for that which has been your delight.'"

17. Faith and Doubt

Just as joy and sorrow can be the products of hope and despair, so faith and doubt may also be built on their foundations, for, "faith", said St. Paul, "is the substance of things hoped for".

Faith, or the lack of it, is a measure of our trust. If we trust implicitly, then our faith cannot be shaken. We may, nonetheless, put our faith in unworthy causes, trusting in something that is unstable, as did the man who constructed his house on a foundation of sand. Throughout history men have placed their confidence in power, in princes, in riches and in their own strength or wisdom, and all these things have failed them. True faith must be founded on truth and, therefore, on God, and because our knowledge of God can only be partial, our faith, however strong, can never be absolute.

Strangely enough, it is because we feel doubts that strong faith is built up. Certainty has no need of either faith or doubt, but we cannot possess certainty while we are on earth. It is not wrong to question our beliefs. In this way we test and develop the faith we need to carry us through life. But it is a poor sort of faith which merely echoes the beliefs of our parents or teachers; a feeble religion which is only practised because it is fashionable to hold such opinions.

Faith must include a certain amount of doubt. That very doubt challenges us and enables us to put our faith into practice. Because there is no guarantee that we shall achieve our goal, we have the more cause for rejoicing when we do so. Every day brings its own quota of uncertainty. Even the weather, despite the careful predictions of forecasters, can bring surprises, welcome or otherwise. Indeed, how dull life would be if every event was mapped out for us in exact detail beforehand. And, because we do not know what measure of joy or sorrow awaits us in the day ahead, we need faith to venture along its paths. A well-known morning hymn declares,

> doubt of what it holds in store
> makes us crave Thine aid the more.

In life nothing at all is a hundred per cent certain. We do not even know whether the things we feel, see, taste or hear are bringing identical experiences to us all. We cannot, for instance, be certain that the green colouring of a leaf conveys to our neighbour exactly the same impression as it does to us. We could only be sure of this were it possible to enter his body and see through his eyes. Sometimes events, past or present, seem to take on a dream-like quality. Are they as they appear, or is it an illusion? Mirages in the desert can certainly be deceptive, even to the most seasoned travellers. There have been those who have said that all of life is illusory; that things can exist only because we are aware of them. A story is told of a man who dreamed so vividly that he was a lizard, that when he awoke he could not decide whether he was a lizard dreaming of being a man, or a man who had dreamed of being a lizard. Life is

transitory and often confusing; so real to us in the
present moment, so shadowy when we look before and
after. Shakespeare summed it up in Prospero's words:

> ... The cloud-capp'd towers, the gorgeous palaces,
> The solemn temples, the great globe itself,
> Yea, all which it inherit, shall dissolve,
> And, like this insubstantial pageant faded,
> Leave not a rack behind. We are such stuff
> As dreams are made on; and our little life
> Is rounded with a sleep.

But, if we believe that life has meaning and purpose and
that we have a reason for being, then it is for us to
consider what it is that we believe to be true and set out
to seek it. This quest for truth is the way in which we
will find our own faith. We shall obviously encounter
doubts along the way, and we must consider them and
deal with them, honestly and patiently. "The road", as
Tolkien said, "goes ever on and on", but we must
continue to travel along it holding fast to the faith we
possess. These words, taken from the teaching of the
Buddha, are worth considering and will provide us with
guidance for our journey:

> Believe nothing because a wise man said it.
> Believe nothing because the belief is
> generally held.
> Believe nothing because it is written in
> ancient books.
> Believe nothing because it is said to be
> of divine origin.
> Believe nothing because someone else
> believes it.
> But believe only that you yourself judge
> to be true.

18. Active and Passive

All that is on earth is in perpetual motion; day merges into night, night into day, clouds sweep across the sky in ever-changing patterns, plant and animal life evolves through endless cycles of birth and death, tides ebb and flow thrusting masses of shingle backwards and forwards over the sea bed, grinding it slowly and relentlessly into sand, while air currents continually change atmospheric pressure and temperature. We are sharply aware of much of this movement around us, but there is some which is so slow as to be almost imperceptible. We know that the earth spins on its axis, but we do not feel this motion. We look at a mountain and it appears immovable, yet even something as inanimate as this does not remain constant for ever; gradually the hard rock will split and erode, though perhaps a million years would have to elapse before we were able to perceive any significant change. But nothing can be said to be truly static. Even after death, chemical changes continue in the body.

If, then, we are to compare active with passive, it would be more accurate to consider active as ebullient rather than moving; passive as unresisting rather than inert. Both states involve movement, but in a different way. When we are passive, we allow things to happen, when active we cause them to happen. In each case the fact of our being there enables something to take place.

It has often been supposed that the more active the life we lead, the more creditable it will be. This is not necessarily so. Of course, it is good to be industrious and to use our skills and talents as best we may, but it is possible to so fill our lives with trivialities and mundane duties that we lose sight of all that is worthwhile. Mary and Martha had very different priorities, and it was Mary who "chose the better part", finding time to listen to the teaching of Jesus, while her sister, engrossed in household chores, remained absent.

It always distressed Wordsworth that so many of his contemporaries were oblivious to the beauties of nature which meant so much to him:

> The world is too much with us; late and soon,
> Getting and spending, we lay waste our powers:
> Little we see in Nature that is ours.

W. H. Davies expressed a similar thought.

> A poor life this if, full of care,
> We have no time to stand and stare.

To be still, to give ourselves time to observe, to think and to absorb the peace and beauty that is around us, is not wasteful indolence. A time of quiet meditation will bring us closer to God than all our restless activity and earnest study. "Be still, and know that I am God", says the psalm.

A wise man once declared that the more his pressure of work increased, the more necessary it was for him to set aside part of each day for prayer. It is true that sometimes we feel that pressing and urgent work may, in itself, be a prayer; for example, working to free the injured after some disaster. The saying, 'labore est orare – to work is to pray' may be justified in such a case. Nonetheless, it is also true that when we are especially busy we have the more need to leave some time for prayer.

Both work and prayer are forms of service to God; the one active and the other passive. Both are of great value and both have their place. The dedicated service of the nurse is no more important than the devout prayers of the nun.

I think that sometimes, though, we fail to recognise the power of the quieter and more passive way of life. Milton grieved when he lost his sight and could no longer exercise his great talent for writing, but he came to understand that "they also serve who only stand and wait". The passive resistance movements advocated by Gandhi and Martin Luther King proved that there are times when more is achieved in the long-term by non-violence than by rebellion and riot. If we consider nature, we notice that the most delicate of plants are able to stand up to storms and adverse weather conditions, because they bend with the wind instead of trying to resist it. Few flowers are more fragile than poppies, harebells and snowdrops on their frail, slender stems, yet they will survive a gale when strong, sturdy plants and thick tree branches are broken and crushed to the ground.

Perhaps the most passive and yielding substance on earth is water, yet it can also be the most positive and powerful of all forces. A Chinese philosopher of the 11th century recognised this and wrote these words:

Of all the elements, the sage should take Water
                              as his preceptor.
Water is yielding, but all-conquering. Water
                              extinguishes Fire,
Or, finding itself likely to be defeated, escapes
                              as steam and re-forms.
Water washes away soft Earth, or, when
        confronted by rocks, seeks a way round.
Water corrodes Iron till it crumbles to dust;
                    it saturates the atmosphere
So that Wind dies. Water gives way to obstacles
                              with deceptive humility,
For no power can prevent it following its
                    destined course to the sea.
Water conquers by yielding; it never attacks,
                    but always wins the last battle.
The sage who makes himself as Water is
distinguished for his humility;
He embraces passivity, acts from non-action
                    and conquers the world.

Tao Cheng

19. Gold or Silver?

There is a legend of a strange and beautiful shield which hung suspended from the branches of a tree, glinting in the sunlight. Two knights approached from opposite directions and, meeting at the tree, gazed in wonder at it. "Who can own so fair a shield of gold", mused one. "It must be worth a fortune". "Silver you mean, of course", replied the other. "It is fashioned of purest silver". Upon which they began to argue fiercely as to whether it was indeed made of silver or of gold. So vehement was each that he was right, that they grew angry and were on the point of coming to blows, when a third knight came on to the scene and they appealed to him to arbitrate. He said nothing, but stepping up to the tree, turned the shield so that each could see its opposite side. One was silver and one of gold. Truth does not always 'stare us in the face'. So often we entirely fail to see the other's side in an argument.

When dealing with numbers we are accustomed to using the decimal system and thinking in terms of hundreds, tens and units. In recent years, however, with the invention of computers, it has become necessary to teach children to understand the binary scale and the employment of number bases other than 10. Consequently, even quite young children will have no difficulty in seeing that when using base 5, for instance, it is correct to say both that 2+2=4 and 2+3=10. Such reasoning to many an older person is completely incomprehensible. Perhaps we may compare this to the way we so often look at life, seeing it in preconceived terms and failing to realise that there are other dimensions, less familiar but, nonetheless, equally valid and true.

When we are considering the apparent paradoxes in life, we are in a similar position. It is all too easy to form a dogmatic opinion and feel that we understand clearly, without realising that the evidence we possess is but partial. We see in part, we understand in part, said St. Paul, as though "through a glass, darkly", and this is not enough for us to be able to claim complete enlightenment about the purpose of the universe and our own place in it.

I have tried to show in the foregoing pages that many aspects of life which, at first sight, would seem to be diametrically opposed are, in fact, necessary components of each other. We must, though, beware of over-simplification. Because there is a balance between gravity and centrifugal force the planets are enabled to maintain their courses, positive and negative work together to bring about light, to gain life we must pass through the stage of death, evil must be worked upon to produce good; but in all these situations, where one combines with another to create a third, there are many conditions and complications before a perfect result can be achieved. All artists know that in the merging and blending of colours it is all-important to use the correct proportions of each.

Many errors have been made in the past because of imperfect knowledge. It is true that 'a little learning is a dangerous thing'. By way of illustration there is the well-known story of the blind men and the elephant. Wishing to know more about this fabulous beast, they each ventured to touch it, but since all felt a different part of the creature, they were unable to reach a unanimous opinion, believing it variously to resemble a fan, a rope, a tree or a wall. However learned we may become, we must still admit to the limitations of human understanding.

When we observe the evolutionary processes on earth, it is apparent that no final stage is ever reached. The flower matures to perfection, but must go on to decay before the seed can reach fruition, and this, in its turn, must be broken down in the earth to allow the growing plant to emerge.

As we seek to understand life, it is as if we are in the process of solving a jigsaw puzzle. We have fitted many pieces into place, some perhaps wrongly, but the whole picture cannot be revealed until the task is completed. When we consider the many-faceted qualities that make up life, and how they can seem to be so variable and interchangeable, one fact begins to emerge. The only thing that can never be altered and that remains absolute is truth. Truth is God, and therefore knowledge of the truth will reveal God to us. In our search for life's meaning, truth is the ultimate goal. There is an ancient prayer which says,

> From the cowardice that shrinks from new truth,
> from the laziness that is content with half truths,
> from the arrogance that thinks it knows all truth,
> O God of Truth, deliver us.

Ultimately we shall find that there is a wholeness and a

unity to which the truth will lead us:

> For All is One, and All are part,
> And not apart, as they seem to be:
> And the blood of Life has a single heart
> Beating through God, the clod, and thee.
>
> *Anon.*

The problem for us is that we often fail to recognise truth. As we are warned in the Bible, we may already possess that for which we seek and be ignorant of it. How many of us have, perhaps, "entertained angels unawares"?

It is for us to continue our quest and, in seeking, build up an increase of knowledge and understanding which, it seems, will go on into infinity. We express our belief in this in the doxology:

> Glory be to the Father, and to the Son, and to the
> Holy Ghost,
> As it was in the beginning, is now, and ever
> shall be:
> World without end.

The world, in the form that we know it, will in a sense end one day, either through the irresponsible actions of man, or by the natural cooling down of the sun, but because the elements and chemicals and all that makes life possible cannot be destroyed, they will, through eons of time to come, reform and continue to be. In effect, nothing has either an end or a beginning. All must begin in God and return to Him. In the words of the hymn:

> Christ is the end, for Christ is the beginning,
> Christ is the beginning, for the end is Christ.